Breaking the Sound Barrier

Breaking the Sound Barrier

an argument for mainstream literary music

John Winsor

Writer's Showcase
New York Lincoln Shanghai

Breaking the Sound Barrier
an argument for mainstream literary music

Writer's Showcase
an imprint of iUniverse, Inc.

For information address:
iUniverse
2021 Pine Lake Road, Suite 100
Lincoln, NE 68512
www.iuniverse.com

ISBN: 0-595-24998-1

Printed in the United States of America

for Jeanette—truly my better half.

CONTENTS

ix

ACKNOWLEDGEMENTS

My wife, Jeanette, provided unwavering support and useful criticism in the preparation of this book. As its first reader, she had the dubious honor of winnowing out many of its typographical errors. Jeanette has also put up with me for 30 years—a remarkable achievement in itself. We've performed together and talked about music so much that I cannot always readily distinguish her ideas from my own.

Kile Smith, Curator of the Edwin A. Fleisher Collection of Orchestral Music at the Free Library of Philadelphia, patiently slogged through an early, crude version of *Breaking the Sound Barrier* and later read the first complete draft. Kile, who is also a composer, provided several insightful comments that helped me rethink and refine various passages throughout the book.

Diana Deutsch, Professor of Psychology at the University of California, San Diego, graciously consented to read the first draft. Her encouragement and technical advice have been invaluable. Even more important than her comments, though, was the information that I found in her book, *The Psychology of Music*. Several of her findings and those of her colleagues are essential components of my argument.

THE GIST OF IT

During the 20th Century, emphasis shifted from the performance of new works by living composers to the performance of literary masterpieces from the distant past. Although the number of skilled composers has grown substantially, our performance opportunities have dwindled to occasional token overtures on concerts. Most new American literary music is performed in under-publicized chamber music settings on college campuses and in churches and museums. Consequently, the public is largely unaware of its existence. I intend to explain why the shift away from the mainstream literary model toward modernism and postmodernism has been a mistake and to suggest some remedial action for getting back on track. While I'm laying out the evidence, I'll also settle two major musical controversies by defining music and by proving that there are genuine qualitative differences between individual pieces, styles, and historic periods.

If you've adopted the dogmatic postmodern belief that qualitative judgment in the arts is a purely subjective matter, then you're in the majority. I intend to persuade you, however, that the majority is mistaken. I invite you to accept a challenge: Please carefully weigh the evidence that I've assembled and then refute my conclusions—not with a simple "knee jerk," but with an alternative explanation for that evidence. But be forewarned: The case I've constructed is sturdy. On the other hand, if you believe that there is a genuine qualitative difference between musical works, I invite you to read my argument because it will provide ammunition to support your belief.

Part of my training as a composer has been the study of recognized masterpieces from music history. It has been quite an enlightening process. I learned from J. S. Bach that every note should fit its context both horizontally and vertically. I learned from Mozart that an apparently simple idea can be remarkably powerful when it is developed logically, from Stravinsky and Debussy that the orchestra provides a stunning palette of timbres, from Schoenberg that alternative musical languages are possible. Above all, I've learned that every choice a master composer makes serves a carefully reasoned purpose.

It has long been intuitively apparent to me that some pieces of music are better than others, but many people consider such qualitative judgment in the arts to be purely subjective. This is a particularly important issue right now because a great deal of bad music is being performed and a great deal of good music isn't. But the extraordinary complexity of this topic makes rational debate very nearly impossible. Arguments about musical aesthetics usually degenerate into "shouting matches" in which the parties simply "agree to disagree." The issue is further complicated by the postmodern assertion that everything is a matter of opinion, that we cannot know the objective world, that each of us resides in a unique and independently constructed universe.

So, how does one present a convincing case for legitimate qualitative judgment in music? Because there are many interdependent factors involved, the required line of reasoning is by no means simple and straightforward. I began with an intuitive conviction that qualitative judgment goes beyond the merely subjective and then sought out the underlying principles upon which that conviction is based. There's no "silver bullet" in my argument—no single experiment whose outcome is compelling. Instead, I rely upon a series of successive observations that can be substantiated objectively. Even so, what emerges during the course of this book is not a loosely associated pile of bricks. It's a sturdy wall of evidence constructed from the historical record and cemented by scientific data. My argument relies substantially upon relating universal principles of aural perception to their very specific application in the process of musical composition.

Part of the problem in dealing with musical aesthetics is that it is generally approached from a subjective standpoint; aestheticians and critics simply tell us how particular pieces of music make them feel. The proper answer lies, however, in music as *object*—independent of any particular individual's response to it, so much of this book will be devoted to the process of weighing and measuring the efficacy of different musical techniques relative to certain universal features of human cognition. If a particular piece of music can objectively be called superior, then the factors that make it superior must be inherent in the piece itself—regardless of a specific listener's response. That is, a composer can *objectively* apply certain universal principles of craft with the expectation of eliciting fairly specific *subjective* responses among unimpaired listeners.

> *Pluralitas non est ponenda sine neccesitate.*
> *(Entities should not be multiplied unnecessarily.)*
> William of Ockham (d. 1347)

I'll occasionally invoke two "reasonableness" tests. The first of these, which is often used by scientists and philosophers, is called "Ockham's Razor." Succinctly put, if there are several potential explanations for a particular phenomenon the simplest is probably correct. The second principle is an argument from extremes. That is, if one process is demonstrably superior to its opposing extreme, then intermediate processes probably lie qualitatively between the two.

In order to determine whether a particular technique is musical, it is imperative to define music:

Music is the use of sound to represent biological rhythm.

Notice that this definition does not account for any particular listener's response to music. Instead, it defines music as a discrete external object. Each listener's aesthetic experience is subjective in that it is affected by his or her personal experience (musical and otherwise), attitudes, cultural background, and native listening skills. For example, a listener might experience nostalgic, patriotic, or religious feelings that are not explicitly provided by the music itself but that result from the extramusical context in which a particular piece has been heard. Another extramusical factor is, of course, the accompanying text, where applicable (e.g., in hymns, national anthems, etc.). Even without such extramusical factors, however, the listener's response is likely to be emotional. The word emotion actually implies movement. One might even characterize a work as "moving." This is completely compatible with music's rhythmic character.

Music does, in fact, imitate life. A fundamental characteristic of music is a phenomenon that I call *dramatic shape.* Biological rhythm is dramatic in that it depends upon our interaction with the environment over time. Furthermore, it is hierarchical in that larger rhythmic events contain smaller rhythmic components. It should not be particularly surprising that music resembles language in many respects and that it is analogous in many respects to drama as well.

I'll use the term *mainstream literary music* to refer to the primary category of music discussed in this book. Because of the impact of postmodernism on the current trend in concert music, however, I'll also briefly address popular music. The words "mainstream" and "literary" reflect certain fundamental aspects of the music I intend to focus on. It is mainstream in that it was, until the middle of the 20th Century, our principal source of concert music. It is literary in the sense that it is performed from written scores and, in many respects, it is analogous to literary fiction.

Music notation has enabled performers to preserve works of historical significance. It has also given composers the means to study the works of our predecessors in a way that was unavailable to the ancients—and that remains unavailable to living composers whose music is not written down. I intend to demonstrate that notation has served as a tool for making multigenerational headway toward mastery of certain aspects of musical craft. It has, in short, facilitated *progress.* Notation has vastly extended the concept of elders and has consequently extended the breadth and depth of mastery as well. This point will require a brief survey of music history with emphasis on the underlying principles behind various historical innovations. I aim to show that literary music has *evolved* along a fairly well plotted course—that it has, in fact, improved and not merely changed. My theory of musical evolution, simply stated, is this:

> **The survival potential for a musical innovation is increased if it either enhances music's ability to represent biological rhythm or increases its efficiency in communicating.**

During the middle of the 20th Century, modernist composers disrupted this progress by placing undue emphasis on novelty. This arose partly from a failure to properly define music and partly from a failure to thoroughly master the craft of their elders before attempting to build upon it. The reactionary postmodernists (e.g., minimalists and New Age composers) relied heavily upon popular models, greatly foreshortening the concept of elders. Furthermore, postmodern cultural dogma has shifted the priority in musical composition from craft to political efficacy. The mainstream literary model is inherently superior to both the modernist and postmodernist models specifically because of its adherence to the concept of elders. This fact—which I intend to prove during the course of the book—provides a point of departure for considering potential solutions to the current crisis facing concert music.

As I mentioned earlier, my argument is a complex one. It requires a carefully laid foundation upon which to build successive concepts. I'll first present some generalizations about the nature of the musical brain. Then I'll elaborate on music's definition, describe its relationship to drama, and explain a bit about the audience's role in a concert. The first few chapters of this book are groundwork. Their content is critical to my argument, but the real argument begins with a survey of European music history. There, I'll illustrate how music notation has served as a springboard for unprecedented progress in the technique of composition. In it, I'll relate some significant historic innovations to recent discoveries in the realm of musical psychology. All of this will form the basis for explaining the short-comings of both modernism and postmodernism. After presenting a case against these movements, I'll explain the inherent superiority of the mainstream literary model and conclude by recommending some remedial action for the present situation.

THE MUSICAL BRAIN

Music composition is primarily an intuitive process.

We have two very different, very high-order thinking modes—one that is largely verbal, reflective, and analytical and another that is non-verbal, pattern-searching, and operating in the present. I'll refer to these two modes as "verbal-analytical" and "intuitive," respectively. Here's Carl Sagan's account of the two modes:

> Human beings and other animals have very sophisticated high-data-rate perceptual and cognitive abilities that simply bypass the verbal and analytic consciousness that so many of us regard as all of us there is. This other kind of knowing, our nonverbal perceptions and cognitions, is often described as "intuitive."…The word conveys, I think, a diffuse annoyance at our inability to understand how we come by such knowledge….The other of our two modes of knowing—the one that in the West expresses our irritation about the existence of intuitive knowledge—is a quite recent evolutionary accretion. Rational thinking that is fully verbal (involving complete sentences, say) is probably only tens or hundreds of thousands of years old….Why should we have two different, accurate and complementary modes of thinking which are so poorly integrated with each other?
>
> The first evidence that these two modes of thinking are localized in the cerebral cortex has come from the study of brain lesions. Accidents or strokes in the temporal or parietal lobes of the left hemisphere of the neocortex characteristically result in impairment of the ability to read,

write, speak, and do arithmetic. Comparable lesions in the right hemisphere lead to impairment of three-dimensional vision, pattern recognition, musical ability, and holistic reasoning....Injuries to the right parietal lobe, in fact, sometimes result in the inability of a patient to recognize his own face in a mirror or photograph. Such observations strongly suggest that those functions we describe as "rational" live mainly in the left hemisphere, and those we consider "intuitive" mainly in the right.[1]

Imagine that you're driving down the highway and listening to a political talk show on the radio. Your passenger, who's been snoozing, awakens and asks you what you're thinking about. You present your opinion regarding the talk show topic. You neglect to mention that while you've been reflecting on Senator Stone's proposal to cut taxes you've also been driving the car. To do so, you've repeatedly calculated discrepancies in speed between your vehicle and those around you. You've operated the car's steering wheel, accelerator and brake pedals, turn signals, and so forth to make continuous and subtle adjustments.

You've probably heard it said that we can't think about more than one thing at a time. But, if the "driving brain" isn't thinking, how does it keep the car on the road? How does it manage all of the subtle adjustments required to maneuver safely through heavy traffic? Clearly, the "driving brain" and the "radio brain" are both conscious and alert, but operating in quite different ways. We tend to regard verbal and reflective mental activity as thought *per se* and all other mental activity as something less than or inferior to real thought. Our "radio-listening" verbal-analytical mode provides this bias. I call it a bias because a great deal of our most creative thinking is provided by our "driving" intuitive mode.

Our hunter-gatherer forefathers simultaneously avoided dangerous predators while catching rodents and picking berries. Their world was a dangerous place. They relied more heavily on a combination of moment-by-moment vigilance, brute strength, and agility than on long-term planning. Now we sit at desks and fill out paperwork so that our employers can sell products in a global marketplace. In turn, we receive money that we use to purchase goods and prepare for retirement. As our ability to plan has improved, our dependence on ancient survival skills has declined. We've been so successful in our reflective, language-oriented thinking that we've incorrectly come to consider "non-verbal" to be more or less synonymous with "subconscious."

Intuition is actually more logical than we commonly acknowledge. A scientist experiences a *hunch,* in which new insights seem to appear fully formed more or less instantly. The hunch is associated with a problem that her verbal-analytical mode has been struggling with for some time. During that same time, her intuition was also at work—searching for patterns that are too subtle for her verbal-analytical mode to notice. Suddenly, she realizes the connection between event A and outcome B—something that has eluded her until just this moment. Her verbal-analytical mode's "inspiration" or "epiphany" is, in fact, the culmination of an extended period of intuitive pattern searching. Once her intuition presents its observation to her verbal-analytical mode, she reflects upon it and formulates a verbal hypothesis.

The intuitive mode's pattern-recognizing process is a survival tool that operates in parallel and in real time. It employs speed and subtlety that are beyond the comprehension of the plodding verbal-analytical mode. It can make practically instantaneous life-and-death decisions. The recent (evolution-wise) shift to verbal-analytical dominance has moved us somewhat "out of touch" with nature. Despite its vital role, intuition is viewed skeptically by our verbal-analytical thinking. The word "inspiration," with its mystical connotations, suggests that intuition comes from an unknown external source (God, perhaps). We consider intuition to be "fuzzy" or "superstitious" or "mystical" or "illogical" and we don't take its ideas very seriously until they are confirmed by verbal-analytical reflection. Nonetheless, intuition is still a great source of original ideas. It's hardly illogical. Its primary "weakness" is that it is non-verbal. Albert Einstein's parents feared that he was mentally retarded because he didn't speak until he was four years old. Maybe he was silent because his dominant intuitive mode was too busy studying patterns to be bothered with mere words.

Rhythmic aspects of thought underlie musical principles.

Thought itself is rhythmic. We naturally group ideas into meaningful and discrete rhythmic phrases. Psychologists call this phenomenon *chunking*. These chunks help us to hold ideas in very limited short-term memory. Consider two alternative versions of a telephone number: 12165551212 and 1 (216) 555-1212. You might think that, although the second version *visually* articulates the number, its function isn't rhythmic. But written language is a symbolic representation of spoken language. When you read the number—even silently, your aural imagination reproduces it rhythmically. Version two facilitates memorization because it visually portrays a rhythmic chunking format. If you were to encounter version one without any accompanying explanation, you might not even realize it was a telephone number. And you would likely read and recite it in a bland, monotonous drone that would make it difficult to recall, even immediately afterward. But if you encountered version two, you would immediately realize that it was a phone number. You would grasp its meaning. And the rhythm of your reading would reflect the visual chunking more or less like this:

Why is this important? Because the brain stores and retrieves information that is rhythmically chunked more effectively than information that isn't. For example, it's generally easier to memorize poetry than prose because poems are rhythmically chunked into lines that are further chunked into rhythmic groups of syllables—often these groups are fixed and repetitive. The duration of the underlying beat remains fairly constant and a meter, or pattern of stresses, is imposed upon it. Even the silences are metrical. In everyday conversation, the meter is not fixed, but the beat is still audible.

The ancient Greeks apparently drew no distinction between singing and the recitation of poetry because it was assumed that poetry was meant to be sung. We still use singing as a mnemonic device (e.g., the "ABC" song). We store and retrieve music in the same way that we store and retrieve data in general. Music that is judiciously chunked and audibly rhythmic is more conducive to human mental organization than music that is not. If we are to perceive meaning in music, we must be able to store musical material in short-term memory. We must be able to recognize recurring patterns in order to establish associative relationships among the components of a work if we are to understand how it unfolds. So, music that applies these principles is more communicative than music that doesn't.

> The evidence suggests that contour similarity is especially important for recently encountered novel melodic phrases that are about five notes long. Contour is less important as melodies are remembered for longer periods of time, as they become more familiar, and when they are longer than five notes.
>
> The familiar versus unfamiliar melody results were obtained with five-note-long melodies...Edworthy (1985) has shown, however, that contour is not nearly so easy to remember with longer tonal melodies of 11 or 13 or 15 pitches.
>
> The way longer melodies are remembered should be a fruitful area for research. Longer melodies must break down into phrases that should be to some extent remembered independently. We know that phrases are in fact remembered as units. Dowling (1973b) constructed melodies using four five-note phrases...After hearing such a melody, listeners were given test patterns that replicated whole phrases from the longer melody...or that cut across phrase boundaries. Memory performance was much better

with the whole phrases…than with the ends of one phrase and the beginnings of another.[2]

The principle that Jay Dowling discussed above indicates that we
remember short melodic figures quite well and that we remember larger
melodic structures as groups of phrases that are chunked. A major impli-
cation for composers is that a theme can be made more memorable if it is
constructed from short, clearly delineated phrases. Furthermore, the
chunking principle is hierarchical. We store and retrieve small bits of data
more effectively by chunking them and we store and retrieve the chunks
themselves more effectively when they are grouped into larger chunks.

You may be inclined to say, "I, personally, can remember numbers and
phrases better by chunking them, so it's a subjective preference and not an
objective criterion for evaluating music." But, in fact, music that is organized into chunks is *objectively* more communicative than music that isn't
because the chunking phenomenon is universal for our species.
Consequently, a piece of music *as an external object* can be examined and
found to be more or less communicative based in part upon the degree to
which effective chunking is applied.

Our sensory faculties use a few simple rules to analyze input.

The amount of raw sensory data we receive moment by moment is enormous. But our survival depends upon our ability to make sense of it all.
Consequently, evolution has given us a set of perceptual principles that filter out insignificant information so that we can concentrate on the stuff
that actually matters. There are significant similarities between our processing of visual and auditory input. For both, we subconsciously specu-
late in order to identify meaningful input before presenting "shorthand"
summaries to our consciousness. Gestalt psychologists posited that we
group inputs according to a fairly simple set of rules:

- **Proximity:** Closer elements are linked together in preference over those that are far apart.
- **Similarity:** Similar elements are linked.
- **Good Continuation:** Elements that follow each other in a given direction are linked.
- **Common Fate:** Elements that change in the same way are linked.
- **Familiarity:** Elements that we recognize are perceived as units.

In addition to these, Diana Deutsch describes *onset synchronicity:* Sounds that begin simultaneously are likely to emanate from the same source, so they tend to be grouped accordingly.[3] When we see a human face that is partially concealed by underbrush, our visual processors use familiarity and good continuation to "complete" the face rather than present us with a confusing impression of something that is part-plant-part-human.

The Gestalt grouping principles help us to establish our most basic moment-by-moment expectations while listening to music. Lines that are close to each other in pitch and traveling in parallel share both proximity and common fate, so we group them aurally with the expectation that they will continue moving closely and in parallel. When multiple timbres are present in a musical texture, we aurally group them by similarity as well. If, for example, brass and stringed instruments are in use, we tend to hear the brass as one unit and the strings as another. Our auditory faculties will attempt to segregate the two and if they are not segregated, the overall effect will be less clear. Once a melody has started, we expect it to continue using the same instruments and when an idea begins that sounds like the start of an earlier one, grouping by familiarity leads us to expect it to continue as it did before. Such principles help us to make sense of what has just happened in a piece of music and to predict how it will behave in the immediate future. In a very real sense, they help us to vicariously participate in the act of composing as the music unfolds. When something odd happens in the music, it catches our attention—even if we're not consciously trying to listen. Our auditory faculties continually search for patterns in order to predict how the sounds around us will behave—musical and otherwise. And if they detect something unexpected, they'll call our attention to it.

Recent psychological research clearly demonstrates that voice crossings impede aural comprehension. In 1974, Diana Deutsch reported a perceptual phenomenon that she calls the "scale illusion." She used headphones to present a series of tones discretely to the right and left ears of her subjects. The pattern performed was this:

But the pattern that subjects reported hearing was this:

The listeners' auditory faculties provided alternative interpretations of the signals they were given. The perceptual principles that were called into conflict are grouping by good continuation and by proximity (Good continuation insists that C-B-A-G form a continuous line while proximity notices that C-D-A-F are the first four notes presented to the right ear). Some listeners, in fact, heard only the upper scale-wise pattern and detected very limited information about the lower notes. Good continuation trumped left-right proximity in this experiment, but at a cost. When voices cross, we try unsuccessfully to segregate them. At best, our grouping is confused. At worst, salient information is actually lost.

Another experiment by Ciocca and Bregman (1987) used two *glissandi*—one rising and one falling—that crossed each other in the middle. Listeners perceived the event as one high *glissando* that fell and then rose and one low *glissando* that rose and then fell. Their conclusion was that pitch proximity dominated over trajectory. This further illustrates the problematic nature of crossed voices in music.

Another study by Diana Deutsch confirmed that when pitch patterns and duration patterns are congruously chunked, we can more easily recognize and remember them. The following examples were presented to listeners to determine which were most readily recalled:

Here is Deutsch's explanation of the results:

> It has been found in studies using strings of verbal materials that we tend to recall such strings in accordance with their temporal grouping...In particular, temporal grouping in accordance with

pitch structure was expected to enhance performance, whereas grouping in conflict with pitch structure was expected to result in performance decrements…In the first, the tones were spaced at equal intervals; in the second, they were spaced in four groups of three, so that they were segmented in accordance with pitch structure; in the third they were spaced in three groups of four, so that they were segmented in conflict with pitch structure…

Large effects of pitch structure and temporal segmentation were obtained. For structured sequences that were segmented in accordance with pitch structure, performance levels were very high. For structured sequences that were unsegmented, performance levels were still very high, though slightly lower. For structured sequences that were segmented in conflict with pitch structure, however, performance levels were much lower.

This pattern of results indicates that the subjects tended to encode the temporal groupings as chunks, which were retained or lost independently of each other. This pattern is very similar to that found by others with the use of verbal materials (Bower & Winzenz, 1969).[4]

A succession of tones will be perceived as a single melodic figure if the tones are organized to facilitate grouping according to the Gestalt principles. We hear three distinct lines in the texture of a three-part fugue because the notes in each of the lines are organized to help our aural faculties isolate the lines from one another even when one player presents them all on one instrument. Good continuation and proximity, for example, lead us to group the notes of each distinct melodic figure together. Other features like complementary and contrary motion help us to aurally segregate lines (via onset asynchrony and absence of common fate). And, once a musical idea has been presented, the grouping principle of familiarity also comes into play.

Our aural faculties tend to segregate sequences of pitches into multiple lines when the intervals are large—i.e., when the pitches don't share proximity—especially at fast *tempi*. Baroque composers frequently used this principle to create a "split line" effect as in the passage below from Bach's *Well-Tempered Clavier, Fugue No. 15:*

The right hand part provides two audibly distinct melodic lines with a single written part. One line includes scalewise descents from G to A in the first measure, F# to G in the second, and E to F# in the third. The other line is a slower scalewise descent (the repeated G in the first measure, F# in the second, and E in the third). At the most conspicuous level, we aurally isolate the two lines by grouping them according to pitch proximity. But other Gestalt principles come into play as well. Because each line has a very clear melodic contour (good continuation), the significance of each as an independent pattern is further enhanced. Other factors contributing to the clear distinction between the two lines include oblique motion and the discrepancy between their respective rates of movement (absence of common fate). The overall passage is a sequence, so the audibility of the second and third measures is further enhanced because we group by familiarity.

Some techniques interfere with recognition.

Diana Deutsch also observed that one-directional frequency changes were easier to order than two-directional changes. This suggests that we expect the pitch to continue in its current direction—probably because of the principle of good continuation. So, melodic lines that involve frequent changes of direction are likely to be more difficult to remember.

Octave displacement of notes from even a familiar melody can make it difficult to recognize. A familiar melody with significant octave "scrambling" is no more recognizable than its rhythmic equivalent with pitch content removed.[5] Furthermore, there is a cross-cultural tendency for the frequency of occurrences of intervals to be inversely correlated with interval size.[6] Combining this information with an understanding of the "split line" process shown in the example above, it becomes quite apparent that large melodic intervals tend to disrupt continuity. This disruption can be ameliorated somewhat by allowing additional time for assimilating larger intervals, but its implications do not bode well for the audibility of octave displacement.

The strongest continuity can be achieved by maintaining a constant pitch because it requires no effort for the listener to grasp the direction of movement. Next strongest is a continuous glissando, because there are no intervening intervals to assimilate. That is, there are no gaps that the listener must mentally bridge in order to connect the line. It follows logically that the larger the intervals in a line, the more difficult the connections will be to make. So, for example, a series of leaps by 4ths and 7ths is less readily grouped by good continuation than a chromatic scale. This principle is supported by the work of Schouten (1962), who found that as the frequency separation between successive tones increased, it was necessary to reduce their presentation rate in order to maintain the impression of a connected series.[7]

Significant patterns require both unity and contrast.

In the following passage, Leonard Meyer explains that both unity and contrast must exist in order for us to perceive patterns:

> The apprehension of a series of physically discrete stimuli as constituting a pattern or shape results from the ability of the human mind to relate the constituent parts of the stimulus or stimulus series to one

another in an intelligible and meaningful way. For an impression of shape to arise an order must be perceived in which the individual stimuli become parts of a larger structure and perform distinguishable functions within that structure. A shape or pattern...is meaningful and significant because its consequents can be envisaged with some degree of probability.

One of the absolute and necessary conditions for the apprehension of shape, for the perception of any relationships at all...is the existence of both similarities and differences among the several stimuli which constitute the series under consideration.

If the stimuli comprising the series cannot be perceived as being similar in any respect whatsoever then they will fail to cohere, to form a group or unit, and will be perceived as separate, isolated, and discrete sounds, "signifying nothing." Since contrast and comparison can exist only where there is similarity or equality of some sort, the mental impression created by such a series will be one of dispersion, not disparity; of diffusion, not divergence; of novelty, not variety.

Complete similarity, proximity, and equality of stimulation, on the other hand, will create an undifferentiated homogeneity out of which no relationships can arise because there are no separable, individual identities to be contrasted, compared, or otherwise related. There will be coexistence and constancy, but not connection; uniformity and union, but not unity. In short, both total segregation and total uniformity will produce sensation, but neither will be apprehended as pattern or shape...

These observations call attention to another necessary condition for the apprehension of shape and pattern. Namely, it is not enough that differentiation and unification simply exist. The articulation must be sufficiently marked and salient relative to the context in which it appears to be noticed.[8]

The following excerpt from Beethoven's *Symphony No. 9* should suffice to demonstrate the need for both unity and contrast:

In the excerpt above, the dotted quarter-8th-quarter figure differs from its surroundings because it involves varying durations and an octave leap, whereas the surrounding material uses only staccato quarter notes and is almost entirely scalewise. In psychological terms, the entrance figure lacks proximity and similarity with its surroundings and its second note lacks onset synchronicity. So, it constitutes a significant pattern and, thus, captures the listener's attention. The surrounding material draws less attention because of its extreme unity. Beethoven wanted to distinguish the *fugato* entrances from their surroundings in order to illuminate the overall architecture of the passage, so he used the dotted figure *only* for entrances.

If he had repeated it continuously, it, too, would have lost its significance. Now, notice what happens when I "decompose" the passage a bit:

I replaced the significant entrance pattern with scalewise staccato quarter notes. The result is greater unity but also less significance. Because the violas enter in parallel thirds with the violins, their material is briefly grouped with the violin material by common fate, so the viola entrance is not clearly delineated from the violin line. When the cellos enter, they're actually in unison with the violins, obfuscating their entrance even further. What emerges for the listener is just a gradually thickening but highly uniform texture, so the architectural message ("This is a *fugato*") is considerably less apparent. My version, then, is less communicative than Beethoven's, so his is objectively better.

The perceptual present limits significant patterns.

The perceptual present is the period of time for which the contents of the present are active and directly available without the need to retrieve memories. Eric F. Clarke offered this description of it:

> Estimates of the perceptual present, which forms the boundary between direct perception and memory-dependent processes of construction and estimation are variable, but a value somewhere around 3-8 seconds is in agreement with a good deal of the available evidence. Crowder (1993), for example, following research by Cowan (1984, 1987), concurs with the proposal that there may be a very short auditory store of around 250 msec, and a longer store, with a period of about 2-10 sec, with the two stores being the behavioral consequence of different perceptual/cognitive processes...
>
> The primary character of the perceptual present is that the contents of the present are active and directly available, whereas memories must be retrieved—must be transformed from a state of inactive storage to current awareness...Further, the extent of the perceptual present is governed by organizational considerations rather than pure duration: although there seems to be an upper limit beyond which the perceptual present cannot be extended whatever the structure of the material concerned, within this upper bound the determination of the contents of the present is primarily a function of perceptual structure, such that the boundary of the perceptual present falls at a natural break in the event structure.[9]

If we combine the numerical limit for efficient chunking with the temporal limit for the perceptual present, then, we find that a typical musical fragment should readily be held in the mind if it involves about 7 or fewer notes and lasts for less than 10 seconds. Consider the following passage from the second movement of Mozart's *Concert for Clarinet and Orchestra:*

At a metronome marking of 8th = 84, a complete measure lasts about 4.2 seconds. The first phrase contains 6 notes and the second contains 7. So each of the first two phrases can be held completely in the perceptual present (8.4 sec) and can be chunked and stored as a unit. Since they are significantly similar in durational pattern and melodic contour, they can readily be associated with one another for sequential recall later. But the third phrase presents a problem. It contains 13 notes and lasts 16.8 seconds. By the time we reach the end of it, the beginning has been removed from the perceptual present to and stored in short-term memory. Mozart's intuitive solution was to provide a chunking mechanism within the phrase. The second measure of the phrase begins just like the first, so the listener can store the first measure as a chunk and shift the perceptual present to the beginning of the second. My point is this: Extended melodic passages should be constructed from shorter phrases, each of which can be chunked independently. In addition, the phrases should be related to one another to facilitate sequential association for subsequent recall.

Scales are primarily cultural constructs.

Much has been written about how musical scales relate to the physics of sound. The tendency has been to claim that consonant intervals are associated with simple frequency ratios and dissonant ones are associated with complex ones. This ties closely to the fact that the harmonic series for a pitched sound includes wave components that are multiples of the fundamental frequency (The fundamental is the pitch that is normally heard). The principle of octave equivalence is very nearly universal around the globe, so it is a likely candidate for legitimacy. The interval of an octave is produced when the frequency of the upper note is exactly twice that of the lower one. In other words, the octave's frequency ratio is 2:1.

Perfect 5ths (ratio 3:2) are also fairly common throughout the musical world, so there may be reason to include them as candidates for consonance because of their connection to the external physical world, but the case is much weaker. Western theorists have argued that our entire major scale is based upon the lower region of the harmonic series and is, therefore, a naturally superior construct. But the case is tenuous at best and probably represents a rationalization based on cultural bias. Although a much older Western tuning system called "just intonation" placed a few notes on or near the harmonic series, the newer "equal-temperament" tuning method should be perceived as a set of extraordinarily dissonant intervals because now even our perfect 5th has a quite complex frequency ratio. So, beyond octave equivalence, the process of scale construction is probably almost entirely cultural.

Through acculturation, our auditory faculties come to *expect* musical pitches to be separated by certain learned intervals. Many tuning systems from different cultures sound out-of-tune to us because they differ from our musical vocabulary. Although there appears to be no special external basis for considering one tuning system superior to another, there are a few things that we can at least generalize about regarding scale construction. Let's try arguing from extremes: If pitches are too close together, our ears won't recognize them as discrete, so we can't become familiar with them as specific scale degrees. Instead, we'll hear them as more or less out-of-tune equivalents of a smaller set. At the other extreme—if they're too far apart—they'll form an unexpressive scale. Imagine, for example, a scale that only included the notes C and G. It could convey so little information that all of its potential for melodic variety could be exhausted during a single brief sitting. Logically, then, there must be reasonable minimum and maximum numbers of scale degrees. On the whole, cultures around the world seem to have settled this issue by establishing scales that contain between five and twelve degrees:

> The use of a relatively small number of discrete pitch relationships in music is probably dictated by inherent limitations on the processing of high-information-load stimuli by human sensory systems. Quarter-tone music might be theoretically feasible given sufficient exposure, but the present 12-interval Western scale is probably a practical limit. Any division of the octave into intervals smaller than quartertones is perceptually irrelevant for melodic information.[10]

The law of affect explains music's emotional impact.

In this book, I intend to concentrate on composition rather than on listening, but these two activities are obviously interrelated. Leonard Meyer presented a very thorough discussion of expectation in his book, *Emotion and Meaning in Music.* A few of his observations will be particularly useful for supporting my argument later in this book:

> Though the stimulus situation may vary indefinitely, the conditions which evoke affect are general and are, therefore, applicable to music. In other words, it was assumed that the law of affect, which states that emotion is evoked when a tendency to respond is inhibited, is a general proposition relevant to human psychology in all realms of experience.
>
> In music...the same stimulus, the music, activates tendencies, inhibits them, and provides meaningful and relevant resolutions. If tendencies are pattern reactions that are expectant in the broad sense, including unconscious as well as conscious anticipations, then it is not difficult to see how music is able to evoke tendencies. For it has been generally acknowledged that music arouses expectations, some

conscious and others unconscious, which may or may not be directly and immediately satisfied.

The greater the buildup of suspense, of tension, the greater the emotional release upon resolution. This observation points up the fact that in aesthetic experience emotional pattern must be considered not only in terms of tension itself but also in terms of the progression from tension to release. And the experience of suspense is aesthetically valueless unless it is followed by a release which is understandable in the given context.

Musical experiences of suspense are very similar to those experienced in real life. Both in life and in music the emotions thus arising have essentially the same stimulus situation: the situation of ignorance, the awareness of the individual's impotence and inability to act where the future course of events is unknown. Because these musical experiences are so very similar to those existing in the drama and in life itself, they are often felt to be particularly powerful and effective.[11]

Recent findings in psychology support my argument.

In addition to the various grouping phenomena that I've touched upon in this chapter, I'll show the relevance of some other perceptual phenomena later in this book. However, at this point, it should be apparent that the psychological principles of aural organization are universal, so they cannot properly be characterized as "subjective." Because intermediate faculties filter much of our aural input, we have limited ability to formulate distinct individual interpretations of the raw data and because the filtration process is based on a set of universal psychological principles, we can posit a few objective laws governing our perception of music. Diana Deutsch made this observation:

> In treatises on music theory, we encounter a number of rules that instruct the student in the art of composition. Among these are the

"law of stepwise progression," which states that melodic progression should be by steps…rather than by skips…because stepwise progression is considered to be in some way "stronger" or "more binding." Another law prohibits the crossing of voices in counterpoint. What is left unspecified is why these precepts should be obeyed: It is assumed that the reader will either follow them uncritically or recognize their validity by introspection. The findings that we have been reviewing provide such laws with rational bases by demonstrating the perceptual effects that occur when they are violated. This in turn enables musicians to make more informed compositional decisions.[12]

The preceding observations about psychological principles constitute part of the groundwork for proving that music has progressed over time—that composers have intuitively accumulated a body of real knowledge about what works and what doesn't. The composer's jargon differs significantly from the psychologist's; the composer's "sufficient motivic character" is analogous to the psychologist's "congruous chunking of aural stimuli," but many of the composition principles that have emerged over the past several centuries have, at last, found support in the realm of science. I intend to illustrate this fact in the "progress paradigm" chapter by presenting a series of musical innovations and explaining the connection between them and various perceptual principles. But first there's more groundwork to lay.

WHAT MUSIC IS

As a composer, I find a working definition of music to be useful. Writing music involves a series of choices. Thousands of decisions go into the creation of a single ten-minute piece. At the microscopic level, I choose pitches, durations, dynamic markings, instrumental colors, textures, and articulations. At the macroscopic level, I decide whether to use one of the traditional forms or something of my own invention. Without a clear basis for making and evaluating these decisions, my writing would lack direction. Without at least a working definition of music, I'd have to rely solely on "gut instinct," but my "guts" could fail me. A good definition can serve both as a measuring stick for evaluating and revising what I've already written in a piece and as a guidepost for determining how to proceed.

I've read many definitions of music, but none that has really hit the mark. John Cage simply defined music as "organized sound."[13] Music indeed encompasses a subset of the set of all organized sounds. In other words, all music is organized sound but not all organized sound is music, just as all horses are animals but not all animals are horses. What kind of organization makes the sound *musical?* How is music distinguished from other organized sounds, such as the recitation of a passage of prose or the purr of a well-tuned car engine? Isn't there a specific class of organization that we recognize as musical? Sir Thomas Beecham said that "music *per se* means nothing; it is sheer sound."[13] Jules Combarieu called music "the art of thinking with sounds."[13] Conversely, Samuel Johnson called it "a method of employing the mind without the labor of thinking at all."[13] None of these definitions offers anything useful in terms of distinguishing music from other sounds.

Some definitions are downright insulting as well as uninformative: Thomas Mann called music "the half-articulate art, the dubious, the irresponsible, the insensible."[13] Henry Miller said it is "a beautiful opiate, if you don't take it too seriously."[13] And Austin O'Malley called it "another lady that talks charmingly and says nothing."[13]

Other definitions are too vague and misty-eyed for practical application. For example, Thomas Carlyle said it was "the speech of angels."[13] Definitions of this kind often appear on cheap wall plaques and do-it-yourself cross-stitch kits. People who coin them do not fully grasp the content of the music itself, just as someone attending a play might be bowled over by the costumes and lighting but fail to understand the play's theme.

Even music dictionaries aren't very helpful when it comes to defining music. The twenty-volume *New Grove Dictionary of Music and Musicians*, 6th Edition omits the definition of music altogether, as do the *Norton/Grove Concise Encyclopedia of Music* and the *New Harvard Dictionary of Music*. The earlier *Harvard Dictionary of Music* traces the etymology of the term but doesn't define it outright. Igor Stravinsky, Aaron Copland, Roger Sessions, and Leonard Meyer have written books that brilliantly illustrate important aspects of music, but still fail to define it.

There are several factors that contribute to this reluctance to define music. One of these is the notion that to dissect something so ethereal—to strip away its cloak of mystery—would somehow diminish its value so that what is called "inspiration" might be reduced to a set of pat formulae and, consequently, music would lose its magic. This position is as untenable as an assertion that the study of astronomy might reduce our fascination with the night sky. I believe that the opposite is true. As we learn more about the universe we become more fascinated by it and as we come to understand more about a musical masterpiece we are more able to fully appreciate its elegance. Another factor that might cause people to avoid defining music is simply the fear of getting the definition wrong. Music is a complex phenomenon tied to the internal workings of the human mind. Its meaning is not very readily apparent. Even music theory books, which describe composition methods and materials in elaborate detail, dodge the definition.

Probably the biggest factor that has prohibited music from being clearly defined, however, is that people—even seriously trained professional musicians—tend to miss the forest for the trees. Introductory theory textbooks usually list a set of basic musical materials. A typical list might include melody, harmony, texture, meter, dynamic intensity, tone color and rhythm. Then melody is described as a sequence of pitches, harmony as a sequence of chords, meter as a pattern of strong and weak beats, rhythm as a series of varying durations set against the meter, and so forth. The mistake is this: Rhythm is really not just one of the trees. It's the forest. The trees—melody, harmony, texture, meter, dynamic intensity, durations, and tone color are all manifestations of rhythm. Aaron Copland came close when he placed rhythm first on his list of four elements of music:

> Most historians agree that if music started anywhere, it started with the beating of a rhythm. An unadulterated rhythm is so immediate and direct in its effect upon us that we instinctively feel its primal origins. If we had any reason for suspecting our instinct in the matter, we could always turn to the music of savage tribes for verification. Today, as ever, it is music almost entirely of rhythm alone and often of an astonishing complexity. Not only the testimony of music itself but the close relationship of certain patterns of doing work to rhythmic patterns, and the natural tie-up between bodily movement and basic rhythms are further proof, if proof were needed, that rhythm is the first of the musical elements.[14]

Copland also lists melody, harmony, and tone as elements of music. I will demonstrate shortly just how these apparently distinct components *all* represent rhythm. First, here's music's definition:

Music is the use of sound to represent biological rhythm.

As I mentioned in the first chapter, this definition does not account for the listener's experience of music. Each listener's aesthetic response to a piece of music is subjective, but the piece itself is an external object. When a composer writes a piece of music, he *plans* for its effect. He understands the potential subjective implications of a given musical passage while he writes it. The composer's craft is, in many respects, objective even though the product of his craft is perceived subjectively. This leads to misunderstandings among psychologists and composers when they attempt to debate the meaning of music. This book deals primarily with music as an object because that approach allows for objective, quantifiable observations. In *Emotion and Meaning in Music*, Leonard Meyer labeled the basic aesthetic stances quite succinctly:

> The first main difference of opinion exists between those who insist that musical meaning lies exclusively within the context of the work itself, in the perception of the relationships set forth within the musical work of art, and those who contend that, in addition to these abstract, intellectual meanings, music also communicates meanings which in some way refer to the extramusical world of concepts, actions, emotional states, and character. Let us call the former group the "absolutists" and the latter group the "referentialists"...
>
> Let us now make a second point clear, namely, that the distinction just drawn between absolute and referential meanings is not the same as the distinction between the aesthetic positions which are commonly called "formalist" and "expressionist." Both the formalist and the expressionist may be absolutists; that is, both may see the meaning of music as being essentially intramusical (non-referential); but the formalist would contend that the meaning of music lies in the perception and understanding of the musical relationships set forth in the work of art and that the meaning in music is primarily intellectual, while the

expressionist would argue that these same relationships are in some sense capable of exciting feelings and emotions in the listener…

One might, in other words, divide expressionists into two groups: absolute expressionists and referential expressionists.[15]

Applying Meyer's terms, Igor Stravinsky was an *absolute formalist* because he believed that music's meaning is contained entirely within the music itself and that the proper experience of it is intellectual—that the listener's job is to understand the relationships it contains. I agree with Stravinsky that a piece of music contains its own meaning, but I'm a *referential expressionist,* not an absolute formalist. Even in the absence of text, programs, overt political or religious references, and so forth, a piece of music has meaning that is indeed purely musical—*but that purely musical meaning is referential because it refers to biological rhythm.* It refers to the rhythmic characteristics of various states of human emotion.

Because rhythm's relationship to emotion is non-specific, however, music's relationship to emotion is also fairly non-specific. For example, fast, sporadic rhythmic activity might suggest either joy or anger and slow, quiet activity might suggest either peace or sorrow. Nonetheless, music is *expressive* in that its rhythmic content arouses subjective emotional responses in listeners. In case your own experience as a listener has provided insufficient evidence, psychologists have confirmed that people not only describe music in subjective emotional terms but also respond to it with physiological changes in blood pressure, respiration, and so forth. No matter how elegantly a work is structured, it must be fashioned to facilitate the communication of biological rhythm to an audience—because rhythm *is* its meaning.

The biological rhythm I'm referring to is of the kind that we consciously experience. I don't think it includes, for example, brain wave frequencies—although psychological research may eventually prove me wrong on this point. The rhythmic activities that we consciously experience are primarily muscular. They include gross motor movements such as crawling, walking, running, hitting, throwing, swimming and dancing. They also include subtler movements such as those involved in breathing, heartbeat, speech, and fine motor activities like typing or knitting. The ways in which music embodies rhythm are multi-leveled and range from the obvious to the extremely subtle.

All components of a piece support its rhythmic purpose.

The following levels are not entirely distinct in real music, but briefly presenting them separately should help to clarify the basic ways that various musical components interact to support the broader purpose of representing biological rhythm:

At the most obvious level lies the *beat.* The beat in music is the (usually) regular recurrence of points of emphasis. At its most basic, a sense of beat can be achieved by repeatedly and steadily striking something (such as a drum). The musical beat is conspicuously similar to repetitive gross motor activities such as marching. For this reason, the beat is usually more heavily emphasized in dance and parade music than in concert music. The human heartbeat is also clearly related to the musical beat.

The frequency with which the beat occurs is the *tempo.* Rapid muscular activity and a fast pulse rate are associated with both anger and fear (fight and flight). They are also associated with playful activities, such as outdoor sports. Slow activity is associated with both sorrow and contentment. Although the connection between music and emotion is quite real, the specific emotional content of a piece is largely ambiguous, although lyrics can clarify the composer's intent by defining a context for emotional interpretation.

Only slightly less obvious than the beat is *meter.* Meter in music is based on the grouping of beats into patterns of stress. For example, a two-beat pattern (duple meter) strongly resembles the left-right-left-right pattern of movement we use in walking and running.

Note values that vary in *duration* within a context of beat and meter are somewhat subtler and correspond to finer muscle activity. These are the values that make up what is traditionally referred to as rhythm, so the fact that they are rhythmic should not require elaboration.

Next comes *melody*. The rhythmic characteristics of melody are considerably subtler, which is the reason that melody is not usually perceived as an aspect of rhythm. Melodic phrasing generally represents the process of breathing. As you inhale, your diaphragm presses against your viscera, creating tension. As you exhale, your diaphragm relaxes, releasing tension. Thus, the rhythm of breathing is the alteration of tension and repose. It can better be understood as a graded continuum of increasing and decreasing tension rather than as a discrete series of thumps. A typical melodic figure involves a rise in pitch that corresponds to inhaling followed by a fall in pitch that corresponds to exhaling. The earliest melodies were almost certainly produced by singing. To raise the pitch when singing, we have to tighten our vocal chords, thus increasing muscle tension. Conversely, to lower the pitch, we must relax our vocal chords. Psychologically, rising and falling pitches roughly correspond to increases and decreases in tension, respectively. Musicians are taught to crescendo as the pitch rises and decrescendo as it falls, even when there are no dynamic markings in a score because increased volume also represents increased tension. There is also a very strong similarity between melodic phrasing and the phrasing we use in speech. This correlation is particularly apparent because music is so often sung. Music, while it conveys stylized inflections resembling those we use in speech, does not convey ideas in the same sense. However, phrasing in both music and speech tend to group sounds into logical chunks because this sort of grouping helps the listener to perceive meaning. We'll consider this in more detail later, but for now it should be sufficient to realize that phrasing itself—whether in music or in speech—is fundamentally a *rhythmic* activity.

Harmony is not really a distinct component; it is, in fact, an aspect of melody, so it is fundamentally rhythmic in nature as well. Harmony originated as an outgrowth of early polyphonic writing (setting two or more melodic lines against one another). Over time, certain vertical combinations of intervals gained prevalence and, during the common practice period, they were codified into more or less standard harmonic progressions. When two or more pitches are sounded together (harmonically), their spacing determines whether their relationship is relatively *consonant* (low in tension) or *dissonant* (high in tension). The correlation between consonance and frequency ratios is quite imprecise, as I've mentioned, owing to the influence of cultural context. Note that the terms "consonant" and "dissonant" are not synonymous with "pretty" and "ugly." This common misconception does a grave injustice to the use of dissonance. The works of Mozart and Bach often employ very strong dissonances. Few people would argue that their use of dissonance is "ugly." The main difference between recent treatment of dissonance and that of the past is that during the common practice era, points of dissonance were prepared and resolved according to set formulae. For example, here's a common practice era suspension:

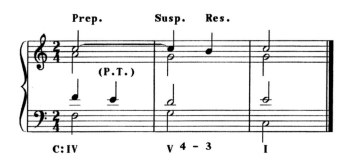

In the example above, the C in the upper voice begins as a harmonic tone—meaning that it's a member of the current triad (F Major). When the other voices move to a G Major triad, the C remains suspended briefly, becoming a non-harmonic tone—a dissonance—because it's no longer a component of the prevailing harmony. In this way, common practice composers created points of dissonance. Once the suspension was established, it was then resolved stepwise downward, maintaining the Gestalt perceptual principle of good continuation. This particular example is called a 4-3 suspension because the dissonance lies at the octave equivalent of a 4th above the bass and resolves to the octave equivalent of a 3rd above the bass. Incidentally, the E on beat two of the first measure was a lesser dissonance called a passing tone. Suspensions occurred on strong beats to emphasize them as points of stress, whereas passing tones were likely to occur anywhere in the texture to support good continuation.

Charles Burney described dissonance as "the *dolce piccante* of music," and said that it "operates on the ear as a poignant sauce on the palate: it is a zest, without which the auditory sense would be as much cloyed as the appetite, if it had nothing to feed on but sweets."[16] This is true, but it is an incomplete observation. More importantly, the dissonance serves a *rhythmic* function: Composers apply dissonance at carefully chosen points—usually on the first beats of measures and especially at climaxes—in order to heighten tension.

There are many other components of music that convey the level of tension. I'll briefly mention just a few: The *intensity* (loudness) is generally increased to suggest greater tension (just as shouting usually indicates greater agitation than whispering). More detached *articulations* generally represent greater tension and more connected articulations generally represent less tension. In addition, the physical properties of different instruments result in naturally varying degrees of acoustic complexity, so *tone color* is also a factor in conveying the degree of tension. The *tessiture*—the specific range of a passage relative to an instrument's overall range—also impacts the level of tension. For example, choosing the bassoon's high register rather than the flute's low register, as Stravinsky did in the opening passage of *The Rite of Spring*, results in greater tension, imparting a rather plaintive quality to the music.

The various components of a particular musical passage, while they might casually seem unrelated, actually function together in support of a common *rhythmic* objective. A typical musical phrase might exhibit several (but rarely all) of the following features: As the melody rises, the intensity increases, melodic activity becomes more rapid and disjunct, articulations become more detached, harmonic changes become more rapid, harmonic intervals become more dissonant, additional instruments enter to increase the complexity of the texture, and the tempo is accelerated until the climax, or point of greatest tension. Then, as the melody falls, the intensity decreases, the melodic activity becomes slower and more conjunct, the articulations become more connected, the intervals between the melody and the countermelody become more consonant, harmony slows and becomes more consonant, the additional instruments "drop out," and the tempo slows.

By now it should be clear that all the components of a piece support rhythm in one way or another. And, if we apply Ockham's Razor, we can readily conclude that if all of music's components represent some aspect of rhythm, then the simplest explanation for music as a phenomenon is that it represents rhythm as well.

Musical structure, like biological rhythm, is hierarchical.

A musical work has an audible overall structure. This is traditionally called *form*, but I believe that *dramatic shape* is a more fitting term, because it clarifies the function of the overall architecture of a piece as yet another manifestation of rhythm. It is analogous to the rhythm of life over an extended period. For example, during the course of a typical day, our rhythmic activity may begin quietly, rise and fall occasionally, and end quietly with sleep. If we were to chart our rhythmic activity over the course of a day, we would discover a series of peaks and troughs in the intensity of our activities. Furthermore, the rhythmic sequence of events is hierarchical: The major events of the day contain smaller peaks and troughs which, in turn, contain still smaller peaks and troughs, and so forth, right down to the individual breaths we draw and steps we take. The overall dramatic shape of a well-crafted piece of music reflects these characteristic human variations in rhythmic activity. Here's a graphic depiction of rhythmic hierarchy:

I'll elaborate on this point by returning to an example that I presented in the "musical brain" chapter: Mozart's clarinet concerto. In Mozart's score, the specific dynamic markings are omitted, but performers are trained to apply appropriate dynamics. As Robert Marcellus, one of my clarinet teachers, said, the musician's objective is to "illuminate the architecture of the piece." The meaning of that statement might seem a bit vague to a non-musician, but to a trained performer, it refers quite specifically to hierarchical dramatic shape. With performer-applied dynamics added, the passage would look something like this:

These markings are by no means arbitrary. The three phrases are all part of a larger hierarchical unit. As the pitch rises and falls, the tension increases and decreases, so performers accentuate those fluctuations by increasing and decreasing the volume as well. Within phrases, the *crescendi* and *diminuendi* (a.k.a. "hairpins") added above represent small fluctuations. The *tenuti* (dashes) are assigned to notes that require special stress. Since the larger unit's shape encompasses all three smaller units, the dynamic levels of *p, mp, mf, mp,* and *p* reflect its broader structural implications. That is, each small unit rises and falls in volume based upon its internal structure (a succession of notes) and the larger unit simultaneously rises and falls in volume based on its larger internal structure (a succession of phrases).

How Music Resembles Drama

The term *dramatic shape* better illustrates the correlation between the overall structure of a musical work and the plot of a play than does the word *form*. While a plot depicts a sequence of events, the *dramatic shape* of a musical work depicts the corresponding rhythmic underpinnings. In the following admonition for performers, Aaron Copland expressed the importance of proper interpretation. His reference to context is directly related to my description of hierarchical structure in the previous chapter. In addition, by referring to the composer as something of a playwright, Copland hinted at the correlation between music and drama:

> A prime question immediately presents itself: What does the composer expect of his reader, or interpreter? I think I know what one of the main preoccupations of the interpreter is: elocutionary eloquence, or, to put it in musical terms, the making of beautiful sounds. All his life long he has trained himself to overcome all technical hurdles and to produce the most admirable tone obtainable on his instrument. But there's the rub; the composer is thinking about something quite different. He is concerned not so much with technical adequacy or quality of tonal perfection as with the character and specific expressive nature of the interpretation. Whatever else happens he doesn't want his basic conception to be falsified. At any moment he is ready to sacrifice beauty of tone for the sake of a more meaningful reading. Every performing artist has something of the elocutionist in him; he wants the words to shine, and the sound of them to be full and right. Every composer, on the other hand, has something of a playwright in him; he wants above all to have his "actors" intent upon the significance of a

scene, on its import within a particular context, for if that is lost, all elocutionary eloquence becomes meaningless—irritating, even, since it hinders the creative mind from getting across to the auditor the whole point and purpose of the work of art.[17]

The structure of a musical composition depicts the rhythmic aspect of a sequence of events in very much the same way that the plot of a play depicts the sequence of events itself. Both music and drama begin with exposition. In dramatic exposition, the main characters are presented, along with some preliminary information about their relationships. In musical exposition, the basic materials—melodies, motives, and so forth—are presented in a fairly straightforward manner so that listeners can become familiar with them. Very often these are first set against one another in very stark relief (e.g., a short outburst of very loud, angular, chords might be followed immediately by a much longer, quieter, flowing melody). If the basic materials are presented clearly at the outset, the audience is better equipped to recognize these main "characters" as they are developed. Their relationships can be explored in increasingly complex ways as the music unfolds, just as the relationships between characters are explored in a play. Exposition, either in a play or in a musical work, provides the audience with a *rosetta stone* by which to interpret the events that follow.

The function of exposition is extremely important because it facilitates the vicarious participation of the audience. This is true in both drama and music. In a play, the audience vicariously assumes the roles of the characters, participating in the events as the plot unfolds, and attempting to predict the events to come. In music, the audience vicariously assumes the role of the composer, participating in the rhythmic experience and attempting to predict the direction the music will take, moment by moment.

To anticipate what events will come in a play, audience members must be able to recognize the characters and understand their relationships and motivations. They must also be able to make sense of the events as the plot unfolds. If the cast is extremely large and events and relationships are too complex, the audience can become hopelessly lost. On the other hand, if the characters are one-dimensional and the plot is completely predictable, the audience may become bored. Either way, the audience is disengaged. The same principle holds true in music. If the audience cannot recognize and follow the thematic material ("characters") as the dramatic shape ("plot") unfolds, the events seem chaotic and the audience is disengaged. Listeners may bathe in the sheer charm of the sonorities, but they will not be fully absorbed in the musical experience unless they can predict at least some of the events.

Not all events should be easily guessed, but unexpected twists *must* make sense upon reflection. A piece that fails to accomplish this is shoddy, in just the same way that a play is shoddy when it relies upon *deus ex machina*. As Anton Chekov said, "If a shotgun is on the wall in the first act it must go off in the third." This point may seem a bit vague, so I'll try to clarify it a bit. If a particular pattern has been repeated several times and suddenly it is altered in some way, the listener's attention is drawn to the alteration because it is unexpected. It should mean something. For example, it might be there to herald the approach of a larger change. It shouldn't simply be a random event. This principle applies to changes of all kinds—changes in dynamic level, instrumentation, tessiture, and so forth. Beat and meter, for example, establish a framework within which the listener may formulate expectations. So, if there is a sudden change in meter, it should have a purpose that can be grasped upon reflection. Master composers like Stravinsky have demonstrated that even continually shifting meters can be ordered and grouped to form larger hierarchical units so that the shifts themselves are expected. Bottom line: Nothing should happen by accident.

There are some important large-scale structural similarities between music and drama as well. The traditional forms serve as frameworks for establishing hierarchical organization of dramatic content. I'll use *sonata form* to illustrate because it is among the most common and it corresponds quite nicely to a three-act play. It is often presented from the standpoint of *themes*. Actually, it is not necessary that a *sonata* movement contain contrasting themes (or, even themes, *per se*, at all), but a typical thematic diagram of *sonata form* might look like this:

EXPOSITION: [First Theme | Transition 1a |
Second Theme (contrasting) | Transition 2]
DEVELOPMENT: [manipulation of thematic material]
RECAPITULATION: [First Theme | Transition 1b | Second Theme
| Coda]

The shortcoming of this diagram is that it doesn't account for the form's tonal and dramatic implications. Considered from the standpoint of tonality, the diagram becomes this:

EXPOSITION: [First Tonal Area (tonic) |
modulation (change of key) |
Second Tonal Area (usually V in major and III in minor) | modulation]
DEVELOPMENT: [modulation through remote keys]
RECAPITULATION: [First Tonal Area (tonic) |
transitional material without modulation |
Material from Second Tonal Area on Tonic |
Coda (extended tonic cadence)]

Modulating to remote keys naturally increases tension. Shifting from tonic to dominant in the exposition increases the dramatic intensity, which is further heightened by modulation through more remote keys during development. The return to the tonic key near the end of the movement heralds a return to a relative state of repose. This interpretation of *sonata form* reveals that it possesses a specific *dramatic shape*—that it's not merely a "form" or "mold" into which thematic material is poured. Its dramatic shape addresses the matter of rhythm on a macroscopic scale. Psychological studies indicate that even trained musicians are not acutely aware of the tonal "distance" traversed in developmental modulation. Nonetheless, the form helps the composer to lay out an effective plan and modulation does provide at least a general sense of intensification.

Works of fiction and drama, including movies, employ similar structure. Virtually any dramatic work can be broken into three acts. In Act One *(exposition),* the characters are introduced, along with their attitudes and motives and a hint of some conflict or unfulfilled need. The exposition ends with a crisis that sets the conflict in motion—that initiates *strife.* During Act Two *(confrontation* or *complication),* the protagonist faces various trials that accelerate the story's pace and heighten tension by increasing the level of conflict, the costs of failure, and the rewards for success. Near the end of Act Two comes the *climax*—a major revelation that crystallizes the conflict. A confrontation *(denouement)* ensues that determines whether the protagonist will succeed or fail. Act Three, then is the *resolution,* in which stability emerges from the conflict. So *sonata* form quite clearly resembles the structure of most plays, movies, and novels.

Many musicians, most notably Igor Stravinsky, have argued that the meaning of a piece is in its structure alone. Mozart claimed that once he had worked out the components of a new piece he could summon its entire structure into his mind in a single, exhilarating moment. If he truly had this ability, it was quite extraordinary—especially since rhythmic events are defined by their reference to the passage of time. If we try to apply the concept of structure-as-meaning to drama, we find that a play's structure isn't its meaning at all. How many people (other than screenwriters) would leave a movie theater discussing the number of acts the story contained, where they began and ended, and what constituted the significant plot points? Obviously the story's meaning is its *theme*—which is reflected in the protagonist's attitude and goals and whether those goals are achieved and why or why not.

Similarly, music's meaning is to be found in its basic melodic materials (characters) and how they are manipulated (plot) in order to create and, ultimately resolve the rhythmic aspect of *strife.* Unless a piece is programmatic—accompanied by an explicit story—we can't specifically label the first theme good and the second one evil and describe their interplay during development as a battle. But we can experience a rhythmic sense of *striving*—mounting tension that climaxes late in the development section followed by closure in that arrives with the recapitulation. So I would argue that, for the listener, it's not important to notice whether the second theme is in the dominant or the submediant or how distantly the development section traverses the cycle of fifths. Those technical details may be of interest to composers and performers, but they're not the message. The message is the rhythm of *strife*. We humans, like the rest of the animal kingdom, survive because we *strive* in the face of adversity. In a sense, life is a struggle that only truly ends with death. So it should not be surprising to discover that strife is critical to both music and drama.

Choosing a specific number of acts helps the playwright in plotting, just as selecting a dramatic shape helps the composer decide how a musical work should unfold. Many composers feel that people should listen to music in the same way that composers do. Composers listen for structural devices just as playwrights follow plotting techniques. But that doesn't mean that everyone should listen so analytically. On the other hand, a listener who can make fairly astute predictions on a moment-by-moment basis is better able to participate vicariously in the composition process than a listener who has no idea what sorts of things *might* occur. So a modicum of knowledge about the realm of possibilities is desirable, just as a minimal vocabulary is desirable for somebody trying to understand the events in a play or movie.

During a movie or a play, most viewers are unaware of the playwright's various structural devices, but they are aware of the moment-by-moment unfolding of the plot. When Todd confesses to an affair, the viewers sense whether Suzie's reaction fits her character. If it doesn't ring true, they'll be drawn out of the story. The same is true in a piece of music. Once the listeners have been introduced to the basic thematic material, they'll formulate expectations about where it's heading as the work unfolds. If the material is developed illogically, they'll sense it and be drawn out of the music. In both drama and music, even the unexpected events should ultimately seem natural—even inevitable. For this reason, most events should be fairly straightforward. That is, there must be a stable base from which the audience can attempt to make predictions. Otherwise, even extraordinary events will hold no significance relative to their context.

Although movie viewers aren't generally aware of where acts begin and end, they are aware of plotting. They're likely to describe a film as "powerful" if the plot sufficiently heightens the protagonist's *strife* to elicit empathy and if it unfolds logically and seamlessly. Conversely, a movie that lacks strife is likely to disengage viewers so that they call it "dull." If the plot is illogical, they'll call it "contrived." And if it's overly formulaic, they'll call it "predictable." All of these principles apply to music as well. In *Music and Imagination*, Aaron Copland offered an insightful observation about the correlation between music and drama, although that wasn't his intent:

> Mere length is central to the composer's problem. To write a three-minute piece is not difficult; a main section, a contrasting section, and a return to the first part is the usual solution. But anything that lasts beyond three minutes may cause trouble. In treating so amorphous a material as music the composer is confronted with this principal problem: how to extend successfully the seminal ideas and how to shape the whole so that it adds up to a rounded experience. Here, too, inspiration of a kind is needed. No textbook rules can be applied, for the simple reason that these generative ideas are themselves live things and demand their individual treatment......The artist-craftsman of the past is held up to us as a model to be emulated. There is a possible source of confusion here: amidst all the talk of the craftsmanlike approach we must always remember that a work of art is not a pair of shoes. It may very well be useful like a pair of shoes, but it takes its source from a quite different sphere of mental activity. Roger Sessions understood this when he wrote recently: "The composer's technique is, on the lowest level, mastery of the musical language...On a somewhat higher level...it becomes identical with his musical thought, and it is

problematical in terms of substance rather than merely of execution. On this level it is no longer accurate to speak of craftsmanship. The composer is no longer simply a craftsman; he has become a musical thinker, a creator of values—values which are primarily aesthetic, hence psychological, but hence, as an inevitable consequence, ultimately of the deepest human importance."[18]

Clearly, what Copland described in this passage was the need to develop the basic materials of a piece in much the same way that characters are developed in drama—to allow the materials to take on a life of their own. This is the essence of dramatic shape. However, I disagree with Copland's assertion that "no textbook rules can be applied." There are many formal "textbook" procedures that appear repeatedly because they work well (e.g., fugato, stretto, sequencing, variation, augmentation, inversion, etc.). Well-trained composers, including Copland, regularly employ such devices. Analysts routinely dissect musical works by cataloging the techniques that were used to construct them. However, Copland's point that generative ideas are themselves live things is important. Each musical idea has intrinsic characteristics that suggest potential treatments and each exists within a context that further reduces the list of effective alternatives. The sequence of events in a piece must unfold logically and seamlessly. Regardless of which techniques a composer uses, the result must convey a sense of natural continuity; its course over time must *appear* inevitable and devoid of artifice. The composer, when confronted by a decision about how to proceed, must select the best route among many alternatives. And that, I insist, is not something that occurs in the absence of craft. It occurs, rather, as a transcendence of craft. Once a composer has thoroughly learned to use all of the tools available, he'll be adept at deciding which ones are best suited to the task at hand. He'll also recognize a situation that requires a new tool. While at first blush the logic underlying a particular decision might seem elusive—even to the composer—it actually arises from the painstaking cultivation of a library of possibilities.

THE ROLE OF THE AUDIENCE

A musical composition is intended to convey biological rhythm to an audience. Musical communication is visceral as well as cerebral. It can even trigger overt physical responses from members of the audience. Some listeners might, for example, tap their toes or nod along during a concert while their introverted colleagues consciously suppress similar urges. During particularly poignant passages, audience members may even shed tears or experience a galvanic response ("goose bumps").

In order to grasp how best to communicate with an audience, we must understand the audience's role: Members of the audience vicariously participate in the act of composition. Moment by moment, they attempt to anticipate events that are about to occur and, upon reflection, to understand events that just occurred in the music.

This vicarious participation explains why people generally prefer listening to familiar pieces. If you already know a piece, it takes no effort to predict what happens next. If you're unfamiliar with a particular piece but very familiar with its style, it takes somewhat more effort to predict what you will hear. If you are unfamiliar with both the piece and its style, it can be extremely difficult to predict anything. It can become, then, very difficult to participate vicariously in the composition process. If the piece itself is incoherent, it will remain permanently incomprehensible. While the music need not be simple or familiar in style, it must be *aurally* coherent. That is, the piece must be structured in such a way that it *can* communicate biological rhythm through sound.

The definition of music contains some general implications about listeners. The extent to which communication occurs during a performance is partly dependent upon the listener's ability to grasp the music's meaning.

Let's briefly consider the question from the perspective of another domain: fiction. The audience in this case is restricted to *readers*. In order to grasp the novelist's intentions, one must, at a minimum, be able to read and understand the language in which the novel is written. Furthermore, one must possess a vocabulary that is commensurate with the level of writing in the novel.

It would be a cultural setback if all literary novelists gave up their craft and began writing comic books simply because looking at pictures is easier than reading words. It would be better to strive for a population that is able to read and enjoy literary novels and comprehend their meanings—an audience that is *literate*. The responsibility for successful communication does not rest with the writer alone. When a novel is finished, the writer's task ends and the reader's task begins.

This principle applies to concert music as well. Thanks in large part to our public education system, most American citizens are fairly literate. They can read and understand most English-language novels. However, most Americans are *musically* illiterate. They can neither read nor perform music (beyond *rote* mimicry of tunes). As a performer, I have observed that other musicians—amateurs as well as professionals—tend to be more deeply engaged during concerts than non-musicians. I have long held that the most enthusiastic audiences are made up of *dilettante* players because they have a rudimentary grasp of the music's underlying structure and also an understanding of the remarkable proficiency of the performers.

This brings me to a point about the term "appreciation." It is commonly taken simply to mean "enjoyment" and nothing more. To be sure, listening to a well-crafted piece of music is enjoyable. To appreciate a piece of music, however, is to recognize its true worth. It requires understanding and judgment. Another misused word is "uplifting," which is often considered synonymous with "pleasant." But the power of literary music is uplifting in the sense that it can elevate the human intellect. Untrained listeners are deprived of its uplifting effect because their grasp of the music is generally confined to what Aaron Copland called the *sensuous plane:*

The simplest way of listening to music is to listen for the sheer pleasure of the musical sound itself. That is the sensuous plane. It is the plane on which we hear music without thinking, without considering it in any way. One turns on the radio while doing something else and absent-mindedly bathes in the sound. A kind of brainless but attractive state of mind is engendered by the mere sound appeal of the music.[19]

Children enter the world musically naïve, but there is no reason to assume that adults should remain so. It is only with the ability to listen intently that we are able to grasp music's deeper meaning. That meaning is truly dramatic; it lies in the striving. And, for a rich, fulfilling musical experience, the listener must strive as well. This is a fitting situation, because striving is rewarded by growth. The full appreciation of a piece of concert music requires some degree of literacy on the listener's part. Escaping from the sensuous plane to uncover the deeper meaning of a piece requires the listener's awareness that such meaning exists. It doesn't necessarily require the ability to read or play music, but it does require a modicum of instruction in the art of listening.

MUSIC HISTORY: THE PENDULUM PARADIGM

Books about European music history generally contain chapters on specific "schools" and "style periods" of composition and include names of their major proponents. They list significant dates and describe specific pieces and events in the major composers' lives. In a way, these details are "snapshots" of something larger than the individuals, something that has its own life, its own growth rings. The major composers have left their marks on the process, but even those we regard as great innovators have produced music that was essentially representative of its place in the continuum. Each composer's style reflects not only his personal inclination and ability, but also the general condition of music in his time; it reveals the influence of his teachers and colleagues, contemporary advances in musical instrument technology, concurrent political and social events, and so forth. I am not suggesting that Bach, Mozart, Beethoven, Chopin, and Stravinsky were unimportant. Rather, I'm suggesting that, in their absence, music history would have proceeded almost exactly as it has; the names of its historic luminaries would be different now but neither its course nor its pace would have deviated significantly.

In retrospect, we can see that a style period usually matures over several generations and is eventually succeeded by a new period that is initially characterized by a fairly bold contrast of some kind. The style matures as composers build upon the foundations that were laid by their predecessors. A succeeding period is often seen as one in which the edifices of the past are demolished and new foundations are laid. But that view is shortsighted, because the composers who launch new style periods retain *most* of their elders' methods and materials. They purge specific traits that they see as too stifling or conventional. Rather than dismantling foundations,

51

they alter facades. A better interpretation of a period boundary is that some specific aspect of contemporary writing becomes exaggerated or weary enough to signal its own collapse—that composers are faced with an impending "dead end" and adjust their courses to avoid it. To make an evolutionary analogy, a new species retains nearly all of its ancestor's genetic material but it adapts better to the environment by adding a beneficial new characteristic or by removing or modifying an attribute that has been rendered useless.

Periodicity in music history resembles the motion of a pendulum. Period boundaries generally represent shifts between the extremes of classicism (conformity, cerebral order, austerity, contraction) and romanticism (individuality, emotional expressiveness, excess, expansion). The basic cycle goes something like this: The younger generation of composers feels stifled by the limitations of the current musical vocabulary. A few reactionary pioneers set a new course, which excludes various stodgy or hackneyed elements of the *status quo*. The fad catches on and a new style is born. It's a bit crude, perhaps, but it has potential. Composers revel in the newfound breathing room. They settle down to work. Gradually, they refine it. Decades pass and, eventually, it comprises a large body of literature with its own fairly rigid set of conventions. The younger generation of composers again begins to feel stifled by the limitations of the current musical vocabulary and the cycle repeats itself. Period boundaries also generally represent shifts between the extremes of classicism (conformity, cerebral order, austerity, contraction) and romanticism (individuality, emotional expressiveness, excess, expansion). The classic-romantic conflict evident in the pendulum paradigm suggests that there are limits to how far music may properly stray toward either extreme. It resembles political swings toward the liberal and conservative extremes—always striving for, but never quite achieving equilibrium.

Most music written during the Baroque Era was contrapuntal, meaning basically that two or more melodies were set against each other simultaneously. A piece usually included several voices or parts, each of which made important entrances in turn and then became interwoven in the general texture. Canons and fugues were very much in vogue. Over time, the processes used in a fugue became fairly formulaic. Each opened with an exposition that included a subject and an answer that was either "real" or "tonal." The order in which voices might enter became conventional as well. After the exposition, one could expect to find episodes, *stretti,* augmentation and diminution, conventional patterns of modulation, maybe a pedal tone near the end, and so forth. The period culminated in the work of J. S. Bach, whose facility and precision were extraordinary. While his great craft was admired, he was regarded as old-fashioned during his lifetime.

Bach's own sons were among the pioneers who laid the groundwork for the Classical Era. The early classicists felt that Baroque counterpoint had become too complex, so they simplified their music by writing straightforward themes with clear period structures. They purged the dense, interwoven polyphonic lines of their predecessors by putting melodies on top and accompanying them with simple harmonization in the inner voices and strong, clean, functional bass lines. Instruments took turns in the roles of melody and accompaniment, but one part could usually be identified as the most important at any given moment. At the time, the contrast in styles seemed fairly extreme, I'm sure; however, the early classicists didn't introduce much that was actually new. The chord progressions used by their forefathers remained completely intact, as did scales, the formulae for handling non-harmonic tones, and the technique of modulation. Gradually, classicists came to realize that their new, simple (and superficial) approach was not very conducive to writing extended works because mere repetition of melodic material didn't allow for a very grand dramatic shape. The older polyphonic processes were reintroduced as features of development, but advances in orchestration allowed composers to maintain the Classical hallmark of clarity. Over time, pieces became longer and more complex. Again, conventions arose. The Classical sonatas, concerti, and symphonies all came to be patterned after fixed formulae. The period culminated in the late works of Haydn and Mozart and the early works of Beethoven.

The carefully cultivated clarity of the classicists eventually came to be seen as too austere, dispassionate, and, maybe, a bit prissy—like their powdered wigs. By expanding the orchestra and refining the principles of orchestration, the classicists themselves sowed the seeds for the next revolution. The new orchestra was a powerful tool that possessed a broad dynamic range and a tremendous variety of colors. The younger generation came to see it as a vast, untapped resource for emotional expression. Again, they reacted against the traditional style. They didn't want to write pieces that were simply representative examples of this or that *genre*. They wanted to write music that asserted their individuality by projecting their inner moods and feelings. They called their pieces tone poems, character pieces and rhapsodies. Even when they wrote sonatas, symphonies, and concertos, they strayed from the generic forms. Works became longer and more lush and chromatic. Composers extended the traditional triads by adding sevenths and ninths. These were not new techniques, but the Romantic composers used them much more frequently. Gradually, they also modulated to increasingly remote keys. The orchestra grew larger and larger as composers exploited new combinations of instrumental color and broadened the dynamic range. By the end of the 19th Century, the scales, chords, and tonal frameworks that had been the foundation of musical composition were scarcely recognizable.

Late Romantic composers stretched the length of the symphony and the size of the orchestra. Eventually, continuing the bigger-and-longer trend became futile. In addition, the emphasis on emotional expression had become overstated and melodramatic. The younger generation of composers again rebelled. They felt that in order to write meaningful new music they would have to challenge the fundamental laws of their musical universe. The result was an unprecedented crisis in music history—one I'll return to in my discussion of modernism.

MUSIC HISTORY: THE PROGRESS PARADIGM

If I have been able to see further, it was only because
I stood on ye shoulders of giants.
Sir Isaac Newton

European innovations have facilitated measurable progress during the past thousand years. The progress I'm referring to is quite specific: If music is supposed to communicate biological rhythm—with all of its extraordinary subtlety—then ideal music is that which most successfully emulates biological rhythm and most effectively conveys it to an audience. So, an innovation that either enhances music's ability to represent biological rhythm or increases its efficiency in delivering that information to listeners would objectively represent an advance toward the ideal.

Late Medieval composers gave us notation and polyphony.

Something unique happened in Europe hundreds of years ago: A system of music notation evolved. Since that time, the Europeans have been able to study music in a way that was unavailable to their ancient predecessors and to their contemporaries elsewhere around the globe. Because of notation, composers were able to develop polyphony; expand and refine musical forms; and preserve, analyze, evaluate, and emulate the works of their predecessors and contemporaries. They were able to preserve the techniques that they found most effective and to avoid repeating previous mistakes. The material that follows is a cursory look at music history with emphasis on the practical implications of various innovations. My intent is to show that the music of a given period is not simply different from that of other periods, as many seem to believe, but that in fact composers have made genuine, objectively measurable progress since the advent of musical notation.

Before notation existed, European music was confined to very short forms. It was primarily vocal and monophonic, although it was often accompanied by primitive instruments. It was passed from generation to generation by the musical equivalent of "oral tradition"—a method that has considerable social value, but that is essentially stagnant. The folk tradition would have continued much as it had previously *and much as it has elsewhere*. Parents would have continued to teach their children the old songs in much the same way they had before. If the occasional wandering minstrel gained a fresh insight, that new knowledge would have been lost—either immediately with his death or gradually over the course of a few generations.

During the 9th Century, a rudimentary form of notation called neumes appeared above the words in Gregorian chant. At first, they were simply diagonal lines that indicated whether the melody was to rise or fall. This system was subsequently improved by including note heads that roughly represented distinct pitches. Later a horizontal line was added so that the relative distances of notes above and below the line could more precisely indicate pitches. Over the next two centuries, this system evolved to include a four-line staff. In the words of Donald J. Grout, "It was an event as crucial for the history of Western music as the invention of writing was for the history of language."[20] For the first time, systematic polyphony became possible. The first tentative step toward polyphony was *organum,* which was usually a simple parallel doubling of the melodic line a fourth or fifth below. This added depth must have sounded exquisite to its practitioners. By the 11th Century, oblique and contrary motion were added so that two lines could achieve a small degree of independence. This enhanced the multidimensional aspect of organum and also laid the groundwork for a rudimentary harmony. It was a significant improvement because it effectively doubled the rate at which a composition could convey information and, simultaneously, enhanced

music's ability to express rhythmic tension by introducing harmonic dissonances. In short, it made music more communicative and more expressive.

Once music was able to carry a two-dimensional message, the opportunity to contrast points of tension against points of rest was greatly
enhanced. Greater tension can be generated when two people sing different notes at the same time. Such tension can subsequently be dissipated by
having both lines converge on the tonic, as in this example of 11th
Century organum:

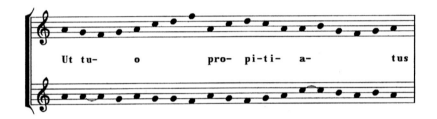

Notice that the two lines in the example above freely cross one another
(In notes 2-3, part 2 is higher than part 1; in notes 6-8, part 1 is higher,
etc.). My earlier description of the "scale illusion" demonstrates that such
crossings impede our ability to discern melodic contours. But late
Medieval composers were not yet sensitive to this problem in polyphonic
writing. Possibly their attention to the principle of good continuation was
limited to the experience of individual performers and didn't take into
account the implications for somebody attempting to aurally decipher the
overall texture.

During the late Medieval Era, monophonic music remained the rule for
amateurs, but professional composers sought something grander. Although
early notation was imprecise at best, it enabled them to develop rudimentary
polyphony. A close examination of the example above, however, reveals that
the principle of heightening points of tension in order to increase the sense of
repose at cadences had not yet occurred to composers. The advent of

polyphony was a significant gain in terms of the amount of information they could convey, but it took several centuries to realize its full potential.

Although pitch notation became significantly more robust during that time, duration notation did not. Medieval composers relied on describing duration content in terms of a set of six modes, each of which represented a specific pattern. This primitive approach made it quite difficult to describe anything beyond simple repeated figures, although actual performance practice was certainly more varied. To improve upon this, *ligatures* were added to the notation arsenal. Ligatures visually grouped neumes and designated which modes were to be used. Although this innovation was quite primitive by modern standards, it was a stunning advance, indeed. It enabled composers to assign quite independent rhythms to the voices. Again, the amount of information that could be conveyed was increased. The usual formula was to assign long, steady note values to the lower voice and more intricate values to the upper voice:

Even as late as the 13th Century, the vertical aspect of music was treated quite casually, except at phrase endings. This is not because people at the time had a preference for unsystematic treatment of dissonance; rather it was because the potential for managing vertical relationships really hadn't occurred to anyone yet. Their thinking was still almost exclusively linear:

Notice in the example above that the three voices travel in extremely close proximity, frequently overlapping. Even if the lower voice is performed an octave lower than written the two upper voices still interfere with each other. This diminishes the ear's capacity to distinguish the three melodic contours. Notice also the fairly strong dissonance of a major 2nd on the weak final beat of measure 1 followed by the "hollow" sounding open 5th on the downbeat of measure 2. This feature shows that 13th Century composers were still quite insensitive to the rhythmic implications of vertical relationships. The fact that each of the lines, if sung independently, has a distinct character, suggests that the aesthetic experience of the performers was probably still more important than that of an audience.

With the 14th Century came the *Ars Nova*—the "new art." The mind-set was much like that of early 20th Century composers who brought us "modern music." Composers were caught up in the idea of finding a revolutionary new path for their craft. This gave rise to the *isorhythmic motet*. Isorhythmic composition differentiated between pitch content and rhythmic content by assigning sequences of differing lengths to each. The rhythmic pattern was called the *talea* and the pattern of pitches was called the *color*. The result did, in fact, impart a sort of textural coherence to their work, but it also impeded the recognition of melodic material. Diana Deutsch's experiment with notes that were rhythmically grouped without regard to recurring patterns of melodic contour illustrates the applicable auditory process. Our ability to remember a musical gesture is facilitated when melodic contour and rhythm patterns are congruously chunked.

Isorhythms and other hidden meanings persisted for some time, but for non-musical reasons. For example, bawdy drinking songs were often buried deep in the textures of liturgical works. This was a source of amusement for composers, to be sure, but the practice was permissible precisely because it *wasn't* aurally detectable. Such hidden meanings represent verbal-analytical intrusions into the intuitive mode's realm. A theoretical construct is applied rather than an aurally intuited one. But by writing an aurally effective work despite such encumbrances, a composer can demonstrate a very high level of technical virtuosity. This could be considered a role reversal scenario in which the verbal-analytical mode posits a theory and the intuitive mode evaluates its efficacy.

Although 14th Century composers showed a penchant for hidden meanings and numerological games, it was by no means bereft of lasting contributions. Notable among major contributions from that time was the realization that carefully planned vertical combinations could enhance the rhythmic coordination of a piece and that the use of altered pitches could increase the level of dissonance at points of rhythmic tension. Consider, for example, the following passage from Francesco Landini's *Ballata* depicted below. Incidentally, this formula is called "Landini Cadence" in his honor:

Because of its effectiveness, this cadence rapidly became a fairly stable formula during the period. It exhibits systematic contrary motion in the outer voices and the organized resolution of carefully prepared dissonance.

Contrary motion is considered stronger than similar or oblique motion because, by moving in opposite directions, the audible independence of the voices is made more pronounced. In Gestalt terms, they don't share common fate. This makes the overall texture especially communicative because it can support the simultaneous transmission of more than one significant pattern. More important than contrary motion, however, is the way this cadence manages dissonance. Notice that the two lower voices move together while the upper voice lags by half a beat. The implied harmony in this cadence is the successive stepwise descent of root position triads on C, Bb, and A followed by an open G-D-G final chord. The 8th note A in the upper voice resolves to G, which, in turn resolves to F#. The F# not only resolves momentarily to E but also prepares the listener to expect the final G—suggesting the merest hint of delayed expectation. This formula clearly reflects a sensitivity to vertical relationships that was almost entirely absent just a few decades earlier.

Besides a readily apparent outline that forecasts Baroque cadence formulae, it also uses *musica ficta* ("false music")—a term referring to the use of accidentals (e.g., the F#, C# and Bb in the example above). It was called "false" because it employed notes that were absent from the standard church modes of the time. To explain how this enhanced the rhythmic vocabulary of the time, I'll have to backtrack a bit again.

There are two additional principles at work in this cadence. First, by having the upper voice lag behind, its independence is strengthened. This is because when we hear two or more tones attacked at the same moment, they are much more likely to be perceived as a single, more harmonically complex sound—an observation that is supported by the grouping principle of onset synchronicity. Second, the accidentals adjust the fairly ambiguous directional motivation of the applicable notes so that they strongly tend toward resolution in particular directions. How? Performers actually sang the altered notes somewhat less than a semitone away from the tones toward which they were intended to move, setting up an expectation about where they'd eventually resolve. There are at least two potential explanations for this phenomenon, so I'll leave it to psychologists to determine the correct answer:

> **Potential explanation 1:** We attempt to identify sounds as specific notes of the scale, but the applicable receptors are stimulated by nearby pitches as well, so an overlapping effect comes into play. The close proximity of the chromatically altered note to an unaltered neighbor psychologically suggests that it's an out-of-tune version of the neighbor. For example, the slightly low Bb stimulates the "Bb receptor" and also, to a lesser degree, the nearby "A receptor". This makes it somewhat ambiguous, creating a natural sense of tension. The listener consequently *expects* to resolve the tension by "tuning" the pitch downward to A. For the slightly high F# and C#, the "tuned" neighbors are higher notes—G and D, respectively.
>
> **Potential explanation 2:** When we hear something (either musical or non-musical), we predict good continuation. Since a slightly raised pitch is shifted toward the higher note, we expect it to continue upward and since the slightly lowered pitch is shifted toward a lower note, we expect it to continue downward.

The development of cadence formulae was something of an epiphany. The Europeans suddenly realized that harmonic relationships could be exploited to enhance the overall emotional expressiveness of their music. They could coordinate all the elements of the texture in order to create moments of exquisite tension and then resolve them systematically. This added a new dimension to communication as well. Not only could the three separate voices in our example above be transmitted simultaneously—each conveying its own melodic contour, but their combined harmonic implications could be transmitted as well. So, cadence formulae represented decisive material gains both in rhythmic impact and in communicative power.

Renaissance composers refined notation and polyphony.

Over time, late Medieval composers further directed their attention toward the harmonic aspect of music, but progress in that area dragged for a while because composers still lacked a notational tool that we now take for granted. Until around 1500, they wrote individual parts in succession because they hadn't yet invented the musical score—a construct that visually facilitates the simultaneous preparation of all the components of the texture. Another great advance dating from that time was the printing of music using moveable type. Although they didn't yet refer to vertical structures as harmony, they did define certain preferences for vertical combinations—namely the root position and first inversion triads. They also started assigning the bass line a somewhat more overtly harmonic role. By the mid-16th Century, the use of musical scores showed its remarkable advantage. Composers could write distinct melodic contours for several simultaneous parts while carefully manipulating their combined harmonic implications. Consider, for example, the structure of this excerpt from the *Kyrie* from *Faysans regres* by Josquin des Prez:

Not only are the vertical sonorities managed with a fair amount of precision, but also the entrances of the voices form a double canon. That is, the third voice enters on exactly the same melodic material as the first but an octave higher and the fourth voice enters on exactly the same melodic material as the second, also an octave higher. Such imitative counterpoint represents a significant communicative advance because it helps the listener formulate rules for predicting what will happen on successive entrances. The temporal spacing of the four entrances improves communication as well. Josquin allows each voice to enter individually, thus drawing attention to its presence and proceeding for a measure or two without masking its melodic contour under subsequent entrances. Thus he gives the listener a chance to grasp the character of each voice in its turn.

In psychological terms, the temporal spacing of entrances assists listeners in chunking the information. Attention is naturally drawn to the successive entrances because each one establishes a new high pitch, simultaneously increasing the density of the complete texture and shifting the overall upper border. So, when new voices enter, their onsets are asynchronous and they lack proximity with the voices that are already present, and thereby attract attention. Through octave equivalence, and the preservation of distinct melodic contours and rhythmic structures in subsequent entrances, Josquin chunked the information consistently in order to reinforce familiarity, thus facilitating the listener's predictive capacity. Intuitively, imitative counterpoint was perceived as very attractive to Renaissance composers. Now empirical evidence clearly shows that their intuition was based upon natural grouping principles.

Renaissance composers wrote more instrumental music.

During the Renaissance, composers began writing more works that were specifically for instruments rather than voices. They became more intrigued by the use of different timbres than their predecessors had been. However, they wrote a great deal of music that could either be played or sung, so instrumental lines did not stray far structurally from their vocal counterparts. Overall, their approach to instrumental color was very informal. Most instrumental music was written for unspecified consorts, so the resources at hand basically determined the instruments used. Performers began grouping instruments by timbre, even though such groupings were not indicated in scores until around 1600—the threshold of the Baroque Era—when Giovanni Gabrieli wrote the first score that specified all of the instruments to be used.[21]

Baroque composers systematized counterpoint and harmony.

As the Renaissance gave way to the early Baroque, composers paid more and more attention to vertical relationships. By the late 17th Century, harmonic practice was quite systematic. Each line in the overall texture still retained a significant degree of melodic independence, but convention dictated what constituted a desirable chord progression. Melodic notes were characterized as either harmonic or non-harmonic tones and cadence formulae became the norm. The resulting music was not less contrapuntal than that of the Renaissance, but it rested upon an explicit harmonic framework. Composers also more strongly differentiated the functions of various voices within a texture. In particular, bass lines tended to dictate the harmonic implications of the overall texture by emphasizing triadic roots.

During the early Baroque, the use of crossed voices almost completely disappeared, indicating that composers had become aware that the practice obfuscated the individual melodic contours of the lines involved. In other words, they became more sensitive to the aural grouping principles of proximity and good continuation. In addition, imitative counterpoint became more systematic than it had been during the Renaissance—enhancing the listener's ability to predict ensuing events.

By the end of the Baroque Era, the methods of choosing notes had become extraordinarily clear and formal. In the excerpt above, from Bach's *Well-Tempered Clavier Fugue No. 2,* every note can be accounted for, both in terms of its relationship to the surrounding motivic content and in terms of the harmony. Bach used precisely duplicated chunks both in the subject fragments (right hand) and in the accompaniment (left hand). In addition, the second measure's overall contour is nearly identical to that of the first but it has *sequenced* downward by a whole step—so the entire texture has been chunked at the bar line. This clarity of purpose assists the listener in predicting what is to come as the music unfolds. The grouping of small chunks into larger ones also reveals that Baroque composers intuitively applied hierarchical dramatic shape.

I've heard it said that the distinction between western music and music elsewhere is that western music is harmonic whereas the music of other cultures is monophonic. This is an oversimplification. Actually, the excerpt above illustrates that harmony is an emergent property. In western music, several lines usually appear concurrently, each with its own contour. Harmony emerges as a consequence of the careful management of vertical relationships among the several lines. Very early polyphonic works were fairly haphazard about vertical relationships because their importance had not yet been recognized, but by Bach's time, the common practice harmonic principles were well established.

Another important innovation demonstrated in the example above is a systematic approach to *modulation,* or changing of key. The overall key of this fugue is C Minor. Bach used pivot chords—chords common to more than one key—to set up for the shifts. In C Minor, a C Major triad is a *secondary dominant*—that is, it's a triad built upon the fifth scale degree of another key. The secondary dominant could have been followed by a triad built on F without causing a permanent key change, but, in the case above, the subsequent appearance of material suggesting Bb Major make it clear that Bach has indeed moved the tonal center away from C Minor.

By using pivot chords, composers were able to create fluid modulations (thus preserving psychological grouping by good continuation). The process of modulation itself heightened the music's level of tension by increasing the psychological distance from the original tonic. This added a new dimension to musical hierarchy: They could shift the entire tonal framework from one key to another, keeping the scales and chords and all of their relational implications intact. Clearly, Baroque composers made remarkable material gains both in communicability and in their ability to represent biological rhythm more subtly and dramatically. Whereas during the Renaissance, the use of good continuation and a set of less precise compositional guidelines imparted a certain degree of consistency to the overall texture, the cues for predicting the music's course were not nearly so explicitly audible as they were in the Baroque Era.

Baroque composers experimented with instrumental color.

Although instrumental music had existed for some time, Baroque composers wrote a great deal more of it. Earlier instrumental music essentially emulated the voice, which was considered the ideal instrument. But Baroque composers used instruments to achieve greater extremes of range and speed than vocal music allowed. Like their Renaissance predecessors, they wrote many generic works that could be played by various combinations of instruments, but over time they made more and more specific choices of instruments in order to exploit their unique technical and col- oristic properties. Freed from the limitations of the voice, they began to create sonorities and melodic structures that were previously impractical. Musical imagination began to overcome practical restraints.

Baroque composers didn't realize that instrumental colors had great potential for illuminating the architecture of a piece, but they were attracted to the idea of contrasting large and small consorts of instruments against one another. For the most part, Baroque composers simply used available instruments and distributed the parts according to range and technical limitations of the instruments involved, with only limited regard for timbre. When voices were involved, instrumental parts usually dou- bled the vocal lines—a process that tends to obfuscate the text and to pro- duce a more or less homogeneous texture.

As the century drew to a close, improvements in violin playing tech- nique began to be reflected in more characteristic and specialized writing for the violins. On the other hand, when wind instrument parts were employed, their parts were mostly patterned after corresponding string parts. Few composers had yet begun to assign distinct and characteristic tasks to the various families of instruments, but they did use wind instru- ments to add variety to the overall sonority.

Although it would be quite some time before composers discovered how to exploit contrasting timbres, the orchestra had at least begun to take shape. By Bach's time, the orchestra usually included flutes, oboes, bassoons, harpsichord, and strings and sometimes horns, trumpets, and drums as well. The string section was a four-part unit with basses doubling cellos at the octave below. In the early 18th Century, the older and more conservative composers, including Bach, continued working in the man- ner to which they had become accustomed. The younger Germans, how- ever, had begun laying groundwork for the Classical approach. In *The History of Orchestration*, Adam Carse assessed the situation:

The composers of the conservative class were content to orchestrate on lines which had become practically stereotyped during the first quarter of the eighteenth century. In their music the principal consideration is centred in the part and not in the instrument. For orchestration on this basis there seemed to be no possibility of further development, and indeed there was none. It worked itself to a standstill. The string part already had its individuality, the wind part had little but that which was borrowed from the string part and which when forced on brass instruments became, if anything, more and more unsatisfactory.

To the Germans of the progressive class…belongs the credit of having first found the true outlet which was to lead orchestration in a direction which has not even yet come to an end. An entirely different function for string and wind instruments, a different style of part for woodwind and brass instruments, choice by technique and colour, accompaniment instead of perpetual polyphony, these were the main avenues which led from the old contrapuntally conceived orchestration to the beginnings of modern orchestration…

Broadly viewed, Handel's work shows two distinct methods of handling the orchestral body. The first is based on a stereotyped duplication of instruments according to type and tone-colour. By the beginning of the eighteenth century the first method had become practically standardized. The process was simple and expeditious: First and second oboes played in unison with first and second violins, while bassoons doubled the bass part. This was the routine orchestration which accounts for thousands of pages of full score written during the first half of the eighteenth century…The system, however, admits of three variations of tone-colour: either strings, oboes, and bassoons play all together, or strings alone, or oboes and bassoons alone…Specifications of instruments at the beginning of scores are often lacking, and it is frequently only during the course of a movement or work that such directions as *senza oboi, senza fagotti,* or *senza violini* reveal the fact that the music was intended for other than a string orchestra…

Much more interesting is the type of orchestration in which Handel uses his instruments in three clearly differentiated groups of contrasted tone-colour, namely, the string group, the oboe-bassoon group, and the brass and drums group. The alternation, overlapping, or combination of these groups provide many more varied effects, and, on the whole, show Handel at his best as an orchestrator.[22]

Classical composers improved transparency and contrasts.

The *Alberti bass,* named after Domenico Alberti (c.1710–c.1739), was a simple harmonic and motoric accompaniment pattern. It elaborated on the Baroque "split line" effect by applying good voice leading principles to each of three separate lines and presenting them within a single line. It maintains a single constant melodic contour—which makes it memorable and recognizable—and it's chunked in congruence with the meter. In terms of communicative power, it transmitted four lines at once (each of the three component lines plus the single combined line) and it also transmitted the harmonic framework, which is implied by the combination of the individual lines. It was particularly useful in keyboard music because its overall range placed limited demand on the left hand. Its continuous motoric activity contributed energy and clearly delineated it from the generally slower activity of the melody. Alberti bass appears in the lower staff of this passage from Mozart's *Piano Sonata No. 16:*

In a way, the Alberti bass illuminates the basic Baroque-to-Classical tradeoff. Once this figure was set into motion, its course was highly predictable, so its use decreased the significance of patterns in the accompaniment while it increased the transparency of the overall texture. Its overuse invites aural habituation, but it was easy to implement and, consequently, it was destined to become hackneyed.

Extreme simplicity was a limited tool for portraying hierarchical dramatic shape. As the Classical Era matured, composers developed an ingenious solution. They employed the new transparent textures for exposition and denser quasi-Baroque counterpoint for development. This strategy served to heighten the contrasts between sections, thereby reducing the risk of aural habituation. It also helped to clarify the purpose of exposition—that of presenting salient material in ways that made it sufficiently recognizable for thorough development.

Although Baroque composers actually developed the deceptive cadence, it was probably used more frequently during the Classical Era. A deceptive cadence was prepared using a V7 chord so that the audience would expect an authentic cadence (V7–I). Instead, the V7 was followed by some other chord (usually vi, as in the example below). The idea was to set up a very clear expectation and then abruptly turn elsewhere.

Although the substitution of vi for I was abrupt, it was logically set up in that the normal voice-leading principles still applied. In both cadences above, resolution of the tritone between B and F proceeded by stepwise contrary motion. The V7 chord was a point of dissonance—implying tension—that required resolution. But convention dictated that the only completely satisfactory resolution of V7 was I, not vi. By using deceptive cadences, composers were thus able to manage the tendencies of dissonant intervals to resolve while still delaying the sense of satisfactory resolution—sometimes briefly as in my little example above and sometimes for fairly extended periods.

As Leonard Meyer pointed out, the result of such unfulfilled expectation is emotional; the greater the buildup of suspense, the greater the emotional release upon resolution. Deceptive cadences are suspenseful; they're unfinished business that the listeners expect to have resolved. Because they're rather striking, they were generally reserved for especially poignant moments.

The process of creating and sustaining suspense applies directly to the concept of dramatic shape. The deceptive cadence was only one of several means of delaying expectations. Classical composers sometimes turned a phrase upward so that the melodic line would run a bit longer than expected before reaching an authentic cadence. They also frequently repeated short figures, stopping them just short of satisfactory resolution. Sometimes they varied figures as they repeated them so that additional information was communicated—but they did so while preserving the salient aspects of the original character. And, of course, they used the tried-and-true contrapuntal development techniques that they had gleaned from the Baroque Era. In short, Classical composers used strategic devices to heighten the dramatic impact of their works by delaying resolutions. They were able to intentionally evoke subjective responses by means of quite objective resource management. Such devices were material gains in music's ability to represent the hierarchical structure of biological rhythm. The next few examples are consecutive passages from the exposition of Mozart's *Piano Sonata No. 5.* I've provided some labels that should help to illuminate the material. Labels beginning with "M" correspond to melodic material and those beginning with "A" correspond to accompaniment figures.

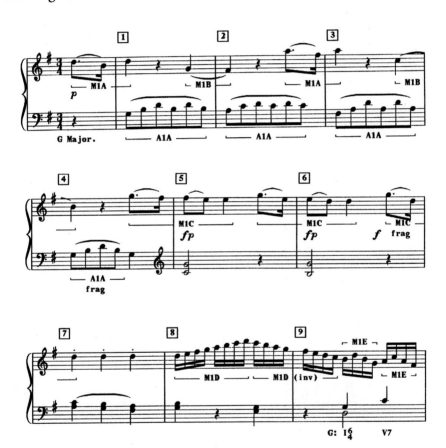

Mozart starts by presenting a pair of short melodic motives (M1A and M1B) that are judiciously chunked to make them memorable. He accompanies these with a single figure (A1A) that outlines the harmony, in the manner of an Alberti bass. It is also judiciously chunked at the bar lines. After repeating M1A a fifth higher and M1B a fourth higher—suggesting an increase in tension—he presents a somewhat longer figure (M1C) that he also repeats, although it is varied on the second occurrence by lowering all but the first note (G)—suggesting a decrease in tension. To emphasize the new idea's role in reducing tension, he harmonizes it using only half notes on the downbeats. He then presents a fragment of M1C, again keeping the G and lowering the next two notes, but maintaining the melodic contour for memorability. In measure 8, he gives us a scale-wise ascent in sixteenth notes (M1D) followed immediately by a scale-wise descent (the inversion of the ascent) and then uses a pair of quick little arpeggiated figures (M1E) to run to a full cadence, completing the first theme.

On beat 3 of measure 10, he extends the opening theme by repeating M1C an octave below the original statement. By doing so, he stalls a bit. He delays our expectation to press ahead into the transition. In addition, even though the material is quite simple and was already presented earlier so that it's familiar, the octave transposition supplies a bit of new information. On beat 3 of measure 12, he returns to the original octave, setting us up to expect something a bit more final. From there to measure 16, he repeats the material from measures 8-10 intact—fulfilling our expectations by ending the first theme in earnest.

The transition begins in measure 16 with a new figure (T1A). Notice that I've used a single label for the entire texture. Why? Because the right-hand material is simply an embellished version of the left-hand material. This kind of texture, which shares characteristics of both monophony and polyphony, is called *heterophony*. It conveys more information than a simple, one-line presentation. In this case, we have a single idea that is presented simultaneously in three different octaves and that includes not only the basic statement but also a variation on it.

To increase momentum, Mozart constructs a long sequence based on T1A. In measures 17 and 18, he repeats the figure exactly but transposes it upward by seconds. But starting in measure 19, he escalates the intensity. He applies good continuation to fill in the gaps and increases the sequencing

interval from seconds to thirds. He sustains this process until he reaches his
target—D—on the downbeat of measure 22.

In measure 23, he begins the second theme. M2A is simply a syncopated downward scale pattern. A2A is a Baroque-style "split line" figure that descends along with it. M2B begins as an embellished ascending scale pattern, so Mozart accompanies it with A2A ascending as well. In measures 27-30, he gives us a variation of M2A. Since it has just been stated, he can elaborate knowing that we'll make the connection. And, in so doing, he not only reinforces the importance of the familiar idea, but he also provides new information. By switching to sixteenth notes, he also increases tension, thus contributing to the dramatic shape. Starting in measure 31, he presents an idea (M2C) that is accompanied by a fragmentary inversion of itself (A2C) followed by a D on the downbeat. Again, he makes a sequence of the idea. He leaves the first 3 notes of M2C where they are and drives the last 2 notes upward by thirds in each statement until the downbeat of measure 34. There he foreshortens the figure, rapidly repeating just the last 2 notes of it in a descending pattern. By using only this fragment, he accelerates the pace, heightening our expectation that something new is coming. He also compresses the harmonic rhythm (the rate at which chords change) and increases the harmonic complexity to arouse our attention.

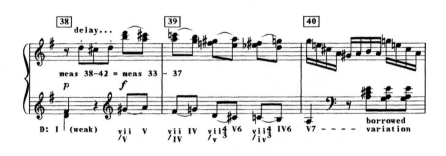

In measures 35 and 36, he gives us a pair of matching downward arpeggios surrounding a 4-note stepwise figure (M2D), which he sequences upward by a second. In measures 37 and 38, he presents a cadence on D—right where we should expect the second theme to end. But it's a weak cadence because the upper D is displaced from the downbeat. He has set up another delay. In measures 38-42, he repeats the contents of measures 33-37. The accompaniment's substitution of 3 eighth notes (meas. 40-41) for one quarter note (meas. 35-36) is somewhat more intense, suggesting that the coming cadence will be stronger. Finally, we are given a cadence formula that lands solidly on D in measure 43, resolving the delay.

Our cursory examination of the Mozart exposition above shows that the Classicists cut away everything but the essentials and, in so doing, they discovered a few new important organizing principles for achieving dramatic shape. Early in the Classical Era, melodies became short and straightforward. But, as the period progressed, they gradually became longer. Composers intuitively applied the chunking principle in order to extend melodic structures while still keeping them memorable. This also served to support the hierarchical dramatic structure of expository material. Small chunks called motives (like M1A above) were grouped into larger chunks called phrases (like M1A + B combined) that were, in turn, grouped into still larger chunks called themes (like M1A + B + A + B + C + C + C fragment + D + D + E + E + C + C + C fragment + D + D + E + E). So, although the basic classical materials were often quite simple, they were systematically assembled into large and clearly hierarchical structures.

Classical composers used timbre to support architecture.

Classicists, in their quest for clarity, brought us a straightforward approach to orchestration. They established the principle that instrumental colors could be used to illuminate the architecture of a piece. They divided the orchestra into three families (strings, woodwinds, and brasses/timpani) and started scoring works so that individual components of the overall texture were distributed to specific families, revealing a newfound sensitivity to the Gestalt principle of grouping by similarity. In addition, they often used the same instrument or an instrument from the same family to repeat a figure when it recurred, thus reinforcing the principle of grouping by familiarity.

Here I'd like to backtrack just a bit in order to compare Baroque and Classical scoring techniques. Baroque composers took great interest in contrasting sizes of ensembles—for volume rather than instrumental color. For example, in a typical *concerto grosso,* the large group *(ripieni)* was a string orchestra and the small group *(concertino)* included two violins and *continuo* (cello and harpsichord). The scoring would call for one or the other or both groups at any given moment. Even when the ensemble included winds, the *concertino* parts mostly doubled the *ripieni* string parts. Below is a representative page from Bach's *Brandenburg Concerto No. 2.* In it, the *concertino* includes trumpet in F, flute, oboe, violin and *continuo:*

Notice that, except for the trumpet, the *concertino* instruments simply doubled the *ripieni* instruments. Because of this, the flute and oboe timbres blended with the upper strings to form a composite. The opaqueness of the sound is exacerbated by the frequent crossing of violin and viola parts. Now let's contrast Bach's orchestration with a passage from Mozart's *Symphony No. 41 ("Jupiter")*. In this passage, the woodwinds and strings have clearly distinct functions. The material presented by each family is strongly unified while the contrasts between the two are also quite striking. The result is a texture in which listeners can very readily distinguish the textural components. The Classical discovery of this principle was a major milestone in the development of modern orchestration. It was also an important material gain in communication:

Although the oboes and first violins cross voices in the third measure, it presents no real problem because of the clear timbre distinction and because the second violins double the firsts at the octave below, creating the impression of a lower pitched string composite. What this passage illustrates is that the use of timbre to differentiate textural components (grouping by similarity) is as compelling as octave displacement (grouping by pitch proximity).

Another noticeable attribute of this passage is the presence of a great deal of "white space" on the page. The Classicists tended to use only the instruments that were necessary to present the basic material. This made it easier to sort out the texture's components. In this passage, the chunking of information is extremely clear. The strings present two figures—one using quarter notes and triplet sixteenths and the other using dotted quarters and eighths. The woodwind figure is constructed from half notes and a descending scale in *staccato* eighths. So the two major textural components are quite distinct in character. The strings supply most of the motion in the first and third measures and the winds supply it in the second, further enhancing the effect. This complementary motion allows the listener to concentrate on one significant textural component at a time.

A composer would say that each of the families presents a distinct, coherent, and complete component of the overall texture. A psychologist would say that the winds are grouped because of onset synchrony, similarity, and common fate, as are the strings, and that the two groups are differentiated because of onset asynchrony and a lack similarity and common fate. Although the jargon varies, the message is clear: Classical composers were intuitively more aware of the Gestalt principles than their predecessors. As the Classical Era matured, composers learned that listeners could distinguish several different lines at once so long as these principles of clarity were applied.

When Haydn, Mozart, and other mature Classicists began expanding their works in order to enhance dramatic shape, they used the early Classical period structures and homophonic textures to present exposition and quasi-Baroque polyphonic textures to develop them. Another important principle was born: Textures could be contrasted with one another during the course of a single movement. As Leonard Meyer pointed out, shape is detected because both similarities and differences among stimuli are present. The enhanced exposition-development distinction allowed composers to manipulate similar thematic content using different textures.

Classical composers explored the new principle further. During the Baroque Era, there were usually very limited contrasts because the *concertino* usually included basically the same palette of timbres as the *ripieni*.

During the Classical Era, a single instrument was set against the entire orchestra to enhance the magnitude of contrast (one timbre vs. many). The two most common solo instruments used were violin and piano. Because the piano was not represented in the orchestra and because it was capable of a wide variety of contrasting textures on its own, its use allowed for greater contrast than solo violin. That contrast was further enhanced because when the soloist and the orchestra played simultaneously, their parts were segregated by contrasts in material. On the whole, the soloist's part was more active, employing shorter note values set against the slower backdrop of the orchestra. Heterophony was used to increase the distinction even when the soloist and the orchestra presented similar material. The soloist would play an embellished version of a theme while the orchestra played the same theme in a more straightforward fashion—thus integrating unity and contrast.

Classical composers also used the new conception of unity and contrast in their solo works. Most conspicuously, this applied to theme and variation form. A theme was initially presented in a straightforward homophonic format and then repeated several times. Each repetition included changes in texture, pace, or harmony, changes to the theme's position within the texture (placing it below the accompaniment vs. above it), changes in mode (major vs. minor), changes in articulations and dynamics, and so forth. At the same time, the salient pitches of the theme were presented with sufficient consistency to be recognized. Each variation relied upon familiarity to associate it with the original theme but the process was more communicative than strict repetition because each variation carried new information.

Romantic composers improved dramatic shape.

Mozart was extremely prolific, but much of the reason for this was the formulaic mode of expression employed during the Classical Era. The Romanticists rebelled against the rigidity of Classical forms. Theirs was an age of individualists. They continued to write symphonies, concerti, and sonatas, but they often abandoned the fixed structural norms. They also wrote rhapsodies, tone poems, and character pieces. Poetry, paintings, travel, and political figures often inspired their music. In response to ongoing refinements in instrument construction and performance technique, they incorporated more and more bravura displays in their works. They saw the orchestra as the ultimate instrument—capable of extraordinary breadth of expression. As they exploited the orchestra's potential, they also expanded it and codified the principles of orchestration.

The Romanticists greatly expanded the use of contrasting textures. Exact repetitions were replaced by repetitions that varied in instrumentation, texture, and so forth, so that new information was conveyed continually. At one moment, the texture might be a homophonic *tutti* or a monophonic woodwind passage. At the next it might be heterophonic strings and brasses or polyphonic strings. Music, then, came more closely to resemble the natural state of life; every passing day, while it may be similar to other days in many respects, is still unique in its specifics.

The Romanticists also expanded the use of development. To explain why, I'll need to backtrack again. Joseph Haydn has been called the "father of the symphony" for a very good reason. In his work, one can readily trace the symphony's development from its short, simple, beginnings to the expansive and dramatic genre that we now associate with the term "symphony." This was not among the things that Romanticists rebelled against. In fact, they expanded development material in their symphonies much further still. Why? For the same reasons that Act 2 is the longest act in a play—often longer than Acts 1 and 3 combined: Development is much more conducive to dramatic shape. It more nearly resembles the rhythm of life. Making a new acquaintance is a brief experience; telling a life's story is not. It takes less time to introduce the protagonists in a play than to confront them with a series of obstacles that test their resolve. Similarly, it takes less time in music to present basic thematic material than to develop it fully.

Exposition is fairly stable stuff but development is more complex and dramatic. The listener's goal is a point of repose—a return to stability and ultimately to complete closure. By delaying that expectation, musical development calls the law of affect into play. In music, our minds are more engaged when relationships among the thematic components are explored and expectations are delayed than when the themes are simply presented in straightforward homophonic fashion. The often-used "pop" scheme of alternating verse and chorus disengages the mind not only by flattening the dramatic shape but also by relying too heavily on familiarity. That is, straight repetition relieves suspense, so it is disengaging—not only intellectually but also emotionally.

Beethoven straddled the Classical and Romantic Eras. His early works resembled Mozart's, but, over time, he became more interested in exploring music's potential for *Sturm und Drang*. In the first movement of his fifth symphony, he emphasized development over melody even during the exposition. Immediately after presenting the famous four-note motto, he manipulated it in a variety of ways—rapidly alternating monophonic, polyphonic, and homophonic textures for dramatic intensity. Even when he introduced the contrasting lyric theme in Eb Major, he kept the four-note motto alive as accompaniment, not just for coherence, but also to prevent the audience from becoming too relaxed. The figure lurked in the periphery—waiting to re-emerge—and thus it maintained suspense.

The Classical approach to theme and variation form was to present each variation as a fairly discrete entity—often with brief but complete pauses between variations. There were some considerations given to large-scale dramatic shape. For example, the first few variations were generally fairly straightforward to support familiarity and the more complex variations came later. The most bravura variations were usually placed near the end to build excitement and, consequently, generate more applause. But Romantic composers enhanced the genre further. In particular, Johannes Brahms gave it more compelling dramatic shape. His *Variations on a Theme of Haydn* and the *Finale* to his *Symphony No. 4* have large-scale dramatic shapes. He omitted the gaps between variations and ordered them so that they progress seamlessly from one to the next, forming a broad, overall hierarchical structure. He prepared an expectation of repose in one variation and delayed its arrival until a later variation. By doing this, he improved continuity and maintained the psychological sense of striving for much longer.

Romantic composers made music more fluid and subtle.

Romantic composers brought music closer to real life rhythm by making it more fluid. They applied more tempo changes, more specific dynamic markings, and more chromaticism. Ever since the advent of notation, music had gradually become more and more intricate and composers had come to think more and more in instrumental terms. During the early Romantic era, instrumental virtuosity at last diverged so far from the limitations of the human voice that it engendered a new kind of compositional thinking. Composers were less burdened with the technical limitations of performers and more able to produce music based simply upon their imaginations. To demonstrate what I mean, here's an excerpt from Chopin's *Prelude in F Minor, Op. 28, No. 18:*

At first blush, the harmonic implications of this passage may look somewhat ambiguous. The first C is leading tone to the Db that follows it and the A is leading tone to the Bb that follows it, but the piece is clearly not in Db or Bb. If we regard the C and the A as non-harmonic tones, we find that the first beat actually outlines G-Bb-Db-F, or ii7 in F Minor. The next beat is an unambiguous V9 with the F-E forming a 4-3 suspension over the C in the bass.

I point this out not to show how intricate Chopin's chromatic harmony is, but to explain the impact of sheer speed in performance. The *molto allegro* tempo marking tells us that the passage is to be played very fast—much faster than it could be accurately sung. The sense of harmony emerges when the piece is played quickly because the salient notes remain fresh in the listener's mind. This effect is analogous to impressionist painting: If you stand very close, what you see are discrete patches of color, but as you back away, the colors merge to reveal a lake, some trees and flowers, and a woman with a parasol. The overt harmonization (8th note chords) also appears scant on the page, but its sufficiency also emerges at a fast tempo because the first two complete measures transpire completely during the perceptual present. So, because the harmonic implications (ii7-V9-ii7-V9) occur in such rapid succession, there is no need to sustain them; each chord is still vivid in the mind when the next is sounded.

Notice also that the dynamic markings that were implied in Mozart's scores were overtly specified in Chopin's, thus insuring that the composer's dramatic intent was carried out on stage. The second measure is an exact repeat of the first, reinforcing the significance of the figure as a unit and demonstrating Chopin's use of metrically congruous chunking. The third and fourth measures elaborate on the same motivic material, doubling its length and the length of the attendant crescendo and diminuendo and, thereby, giving the entire passage a definite dramatic shape.

The 16ths are continuous except when the chords are sounded. The melody and accompaniment are distinguished by lack of similarity (8ths vs. 16ths, monophonic vs. homophonic), lack of common fate, and onset asynchrony. The motoric energy of the melody is so great that sustaining material would simply obfuscate its architecture. The 16ths are audibly grouped into stepwise pairs. At points where the melody leaps, disrupting good continuation somewhat, the notes also serve to accentuate the harmony by outlining chords (e.g., G-Bb-G in the first measure). In addition, Chopin takes advantage of the melody's pauses over the harmony by using a distinct duration pattern (dotted quarter-8th), so that it is more memorable for later recall.

The steady 16ths and the regularity of the harmonic rhythm impart a definite metrical sense, even in the absence of beat-by-beat "thumps" from the accompaniment. Because of this, the quintuplet in the fourth measure makes sense to the ear but it also imparts a fluidity that was previously uncommon. Later in this prelude, Chopin uses even more far-flung groupings of 17 and 22 notes, but they flow quite naturally because the sense of meter is so clearly audible.

Romantic composers enhanced orchestral color and power.

During the Romantic Era, composers focused a great deal more attention on codifying the technique of orchestration. Classical composers had discovered that grouping textural components by tone color improved clarity, but their understanding of the principle had not yet solidified. Hector Berlioz worked very hard to bring new precision to the process and wrote the first important book on orchestration. Below is an excerpt from Tchaikovsky's *Symphony No. 4* that exhibits very some precise Romantic Era orchestral thinking:

The texture has four discrete components: a melodic figure made up mainly of 8ths and quarters in the woodwinds, a quick scalewise figure in the upper strings made up of 16ths, a series of *pizzicato* 8ths in the lower strings, and repeated half notes in the horns. Each component has a distinct character (grouping by common fate) and a distinct tone color (grouping by similarity) and each is clearly distinguished from the others by lack of similarity and common fate. The woodwinds present the primary melodic material, which is answered via complementary motion in the upper strings. The strings rest while the winds play and vice versa, so they lack onset synchronicity and so that the overall texture at any given moment is uncluttered—alternately drawing the listener's attention to a single, unambiguous event. The horns play a pedal at octaves on E. Because it is a simple repeated note, it lacks significance and falls into the background, serving basically as a metronome to reinforce the listener's sense of meter. The other accompaniment figure—the *pizzicato* pattern in the low strings—avoids onset synchronicity with the horns and, using a quasi-Baroque "split line" character, presents a sketchy harmonic framework. For further clarity, the *pizzicati* never double the horn's pitches. It is also worth noting that Tchaikovsky frequently used brass instruments in open octaves. This helped to clarify brass lines because it reduced the complexity of interaction among harmonics. So, although Classical composers began to group instruments by similarity, Romantic composers—especially those in France and Russia—were the first to fully grasp the ramifications of this important psychological principle.

Although fast, *bravura* playing was most apparent in solo works and *concerti,* it also made its way into orchestral works. In the string passage below, from Wagner's *Tristan und Isolde,* the violins begin each phrase with a rapid stepwise ascending anacrusis. The pattern's use of good continuation helps the listener to audibly connect its low starting point with its high end point. The listener needn't make out the exact pitch content or even the number of notes it encompasses. The upward stepwise "rush" serves as a memorable effect, so that future references may alter the exact number of notes, the specific tonal implications, and so forth, but listeners will still readily associate it by its character:

Wagner repeats varied versions of this figure for 21 measures, gradually inching higher, and finally arriving on Ab a diminished octave above the A that its first occurrence led to. The passage contributes to an extended dramatic shape by sustaining a long, fairly continuous general rise in pitch. The marking "*sempre piu F*" means "always louder," so intensity increases continually along with the rise in pitch. Although the number of notes in the figure would seem excessive for chunking, the pattern can be mentally cataloged as a unit—more like a vector with fixed beginning and ending points, direction, and modality than as a succession of discrete pitches. This same principle applies to *glissandi,* which are heard as "slides" rather than infinitely dense successions of pitches.

There were many other innovations during the Romantic Era that supported both greater rhythmic fluidity and extended dramatic shape. For example, Brahms frequently used borrowed rhythms (triple divisions in duple meter, etc.), but the Romanticists, like earlier common practice composers, consistently established and maintained a strong metrical frame of reference upon which listeners could base expectations. Romanticists, then, wrote music that was more clearly audible, more representative of dramatic shape, and more fluid than their predecessors. So they made material gains both in representation of biological rhythm and in communicability.

Early modernists faced a dead end.

The Romantic Era's ever-increasing chromaticism eventually exceeded the limits of common practice tonality. To use an evolutionary analogy, the situation at the end of the Romantic Era resembled an astronomical cataclysm rather than the usual generation-to-generation evolutionary trek. Composers could simply rebel against the size of the contemporary orchestra or against the complexity of the new chromaticism, but where would that lead? Backward to the Classical Era? It had already reached a dead end. It was extinct, as were the periods that preceded it. The only direction to go was forward. So the 20th Century began with a flurry of new styles competing to fill a profound musical void. Modernism was born.

In 1894, Claude Debussy wrote *Prélude à l'après-midi d'un faune*. In it, he constructed shimmering successions of extended chords. He shifted emphasis from the traditional key-defining roles of chords to their sensual coloristic potential. Igor Stravinsky's *Firebird* of 1910 also shifted emphasis from traditional harmony to colorful orchestration. And Arnold Schoenberg, who, during the 1890's had written in the style of Wagner, wrote *Pierrot Lunaire* in 1912. In that work, he used *Sprechstimme,* for which pitches are only loosely notated. He very nearly achieved his goal of writing an *atonal* work.

In general, composers at that time experimented with widely divergent sizes of orchestras, methods of scoring, and approaches to the task of choosing notes. Stravinsky often wrote simple, even primitive melodic material and accompanied it with exquisite orchestration. Debussy developed small melodic fragments into themes that only slightly resembled their Romantic counterparts and set them against shimmering, pulsating orchestral backdrops without the common-practice tonal implications. Schoenberg rejected the huge Romantic orchestrations of his early years and switched to chamber works that emphasized very complex contrapuntal interplay among individual lines. It is important to understand that this was not simply the mischief of a group of anarchists attempting to overthrow the established order. It was necessitated by the circumstances of the day. The early modernists were, in fact, schooled by their elders. Consequently, the ongoing discourse was not yet disrupted. Indeed, many of the early modernists created works of extraordinary beauty and originality. But what lay ahead was disaster.

RECONCILING THE PARADIGMS

I've interrupted my survey of music history at the beginning of the 20th Century because the events that followed are germane to the modernist and postmodernist movements, which I'll cover in more detail later. For the moment, I'd like to show how the two historical paradigms are related.

It should be clear by this point that European music has, in fact, progressed and not merely changed over the past millennium. Contrary to postmodern dogma, this observation is not the product of cultural bias. It isn't Euro-centric or snobby or elitist. It's just true. European advances in the development of polyphony, harmony, and orchestration and in the extension of dramatic shape over the past several centuries were utterly unparalleled in the rest of the world and came about largely because of their systematic music notation. If there has been progress in the craft of composition, it follows logically that there are genuine qualitative differences between works. Those composers who have most thoroughly assimilated the progress paradigm are also the most likely to produce works of lasting value—works that contribute to the ongoing discourse.

It would have been impossible for Josquin to write like Bach or for Mozart to write like Debussy, not because of shortcomings in their native musical abilities but because of the historical contexts into which they were born. Each, in turn, stood on the shoulders of a successively larger collection of giants. Josquin couldn't have imagined Bach's music because the common practice contrapuntal-harmonic principles had not yet been formulated. Mozart couldn't have imagined Debussy's music because the principles of modern orchestration had not yet been codified. This doesn't detract from the importance of the earlier composers. But the fact remains that Bach was better at choosing the notes than Josquin and Tchaikovsky was better at orchestration than Bach. Progress applies in all other fields. Why wouldn't it apply in the arts?

The historical record has important implications regarding music's evolution. The pendulum paradigm shows that European music history divides into periods whose borders represent reactionary pendulum swings but the progress paradigm shows that there have been real material advances that transcend the stylistic periods. These two apparently disparate paradigms are reconciled by a binding principle. Reactions at period borders tend to purge more than they should—to "throw out the baby with the bathwater." But they also lead to reflection, preservation of the most useful innovations, and subsequent recovery of any significant losses. So history's course is self-correcting.

Far from destructive, period boundaries help composers to identify and preserve those techniques that are truly important. For example, the early Classicists oversimplified their music when they reacted against the complex polyphony of the Baroque Era, but they contributed a new level of clarity and laid the groundwork for modern orchestration. Hundreds, if not thousands, of largely forgotten composers contributed to the process. In a sense, they were standing too close to the work to see what would eventually become of it. Later composers would have to reconcile the two styles—primarily Haydn and Mozart. We tend to remember the composers who arrive late in each period because they've been given the advantage of distance. They're not directly embroiled in the reactionary controversy and the newer style has become fairly stable and orderly—handed to them more or less fully formed so that they can reflect and refine rather than struggle to work out the fundamentals.

The process is a bit like panning for gold. Each period is a single dip into the stream that dredges up a new mixture of sediment and stones. But, with judicious screening, the sediment relinquishes a few real nuggets. These musical "nuggets" are accumulated in an ever-growing bagful of useful techniques. My theory of musical evolution is this:

> **The survival potential for a musical innovation is increased if it either enhances music's ability to represent biological rhythm or increases its efficiency in communicating.**

The second survey of music history I presented concentrated quite specifically on these two characteristics of musical innovations over the past millennium. My theory is supported both by music's definition and by the historical record. Although I can't present a simple experiment to prove it, our short jaunt through history clearly supports it.

THE CYCLE OF MASTERY

As I mentioned in the first chapter, I had an intuitive conviction that qualitative judgment is not simply subjective. But this conviction was difficult to present persuasively. So I constructed a hypothesis to explain my hunch and sought out supporting evidence. It should be clear by this point that progress has, in fact, been made—thanks in large part to the invention of musical notation, which effectively extended the concept of elders beyond those who live here and now to those who came long before us.

The progress paradigm depends upon intergenerational assimilation of an ever-growing body of accumulated wisdom. The course of Western music during the past millennium has been slow and arduous, but the progress paradigm has repeatedly proven itself. It came into existence hundreds of years before the field of psychology. Even so, composers have intuitively refined their craft in ways that have decisively enhanced music's power to communicate biological rhythm—a fact that is now supported by empirical evidence. So it is perfectly reasonable to conclude that composers, once they have mastered the craft of their predecessors, intuit and exploit those techniques that objectively improve music's quality.

In a sense, each composer represents a microcosmic embodiment of the paradigm by studying the work of preceding generations. Once a composer has assimilated the paradigm, he is prepared for the quest to advance it toward an unrealized ideal. Early Beethoven sounds like Mozart because Beethoven had to assimilate what Mozart knew before he could truly advance the craft. You see? There is no quick, easy way to skip the studying and leap ahead. Failing to assimilate the accumulated wisdom guarantees that you will contribute nothing of significance.

My use of the words "microcosmic embodiment" and "quest" might sound a little mystical, so I'll elaborate a bit. The same principle applies in other fields. For example, medical training includes the study of accumulated knowledge about pharmacology, anatomy, surgical procedures, symptoms, and so forth. Medical students have much to learn before becoming competent doctors. The learning doesn't just come from books, either. Much of it is practical knowledge that is passed on directly by their elders. Experienced specialists monitor interns to insure that they properly execute techniques like dressing wounds and setting bones. They correct their students' mistakes by explaining how and why things are done as they are. The process continues across generations, each of which contributes to the medical field's accumulated body of wisdom. An unrealized ideal in medicine is the ability to cure anyone of anything.

In most fields this concept is self-apparent. But, oddly, in the arts it is not. Non-musicians often refer to professional musicians as "talented"—as though the ability to play is a gift that has been bestowed upon us without intent or effort. In fact, musicians invest a great deal of time and effort in learning to play and composers invest a great deal of time and effort in learning to write. Audiences are simply unaware of the years of preparation that culminate in a professional career. I'm not suggesting that talent plays no role. In fact, talent (natural aptitude) plays a role in any occupation. But, no matter how great your natural aptitude, you cannot expect to practice medicine well without first attending medical school. Nor can you expect to be a professional musician or composer without first undertaking extensive training.

The term "masterpiece" arose during the Medieval Era. Back then, young boys entered guilds to study particular arts or trades. They began as apprentices. In that role they swept floors and carried firewood, but they also observed and helped out by performing incremental tasks in the trade. Once they were secure in the basics, they became journeymen and were relieved of the more mundane duties. With guidance and the accrual of experience and skill, they were eventually prepared to prove that they'd mastered the craft by producing something worthy of a master—a master-piece. Guild masters, not untrained critics, evaluated masterpieces because only they were equipped to recognize real mastery.

Many people express their musical preferences without hesitation and argue vehemently that their favorite "artists" are the best. But very few would accuse a heart surgeon of being "elitist" for knowing something that they didn't. They wouldn't offer suggestions about how to perform a quadruple bypass ("Say, Doc, why don't you come in through the hip so the scar doesn't show on my chest?") They wouldn't consult untrained "medicine critics" who presume to judge how our orthopedic surgeons should set bones.

Casual listeners have assimilated the progress paradigm to varying degrees (just as "pop" musicians have). Fairly skilled listeners—amateur musicians, people who've taken music appreciation courses, etc.—have assimilated somewhat more of it than most. Thoroughly trained profes-sional musicians have assimilated most of it. This is because they've worked directly with the material of past masters and they've also been informed by the accumulated wisdom of elder performers.

There are some aspects of the paradigm, however, that come from the process of composing and from direct interaction with elder composers, so trained composers are the only people who have thoroughly assimilated the progress paradigm for composition. The process of composing is one of applied judgment. Part of a composer's training is the study of past masterpieces—essentially a verbal-analytical process that includes memo-rizing rules, studying scores, and so forth. But the training also involves writing in the styles of past masters. This helps young composers to inter-nalize the underlying principles, to exercise their intuition by *doing* what past composers have done. In this way, composers develop the ability to think in the same way that their predecessors thought. Once a student composer can write convincing works in the style of Bach, for example, he has assimilated the paradigm as it stood in Bach's time. He has learned to make decisions as Bach would have made them.

An additional component of the composer's training is musicianship. However, principles of musicianship are not generally taught in music theory courses. Before the 20th Century, history's major composers were also skilled performers. Many were, in fact, renowned *virtuosi*. This aspect of composer preparation has been downplayed over the past several decades, but it really is critical. Composers learn a great deal about what works and what doesn't by studying with elder performers and by practicing and performing the great literature of the past. There are subtle skills one learns about phrasing and articulation, for example, that a young composer internalizes so that she is better prepared to write.

A composer must decide exactly what to include and exclude; he must be aware of whether he's achieved exactly what he intended—which is not simply to create something "pretty." It is also to advance the paradigm itself. A composer's judgment must include both a working knowledge of the art as it stands and an intuitive grasp of directions it might take in the near future.

One of my colleagues said, "Any fool can engage in a game of 'one-ups-man-ship' with music history." But that's not true. Successfully competing with the likes of Bach, Beethoven, Brahms, and Bartók requires considerable skill. Contrary to my colleague's opinion, any fool can come up with an excuse to avoid the task. But the consequence is that he'll contribute nothing of value. One-ups-man-ship is precisely the game we're playing. Every historical advance made during the past millennium was a "one up." As I showed in the progress paradigm chapter, those advances represent real material gains and not simply differences or preferences of style. Like Sir Isaac Newton, we composers are standing on the shoulders of giants. With each successive generation, the accumulated wisdom increases, so the likelihood of contributing something new and important diminishes. Even so, it's our turn to try. To do less would be a disservice to our art. To take the easy path by writing in an older style would be a setback for the paradigm. It would represent lost ground that somebody else would have to recover later. When John Tavener writes imitation Medieval organum and plainsong while claiming that Mozart and Beethoven weren't "primordial" enough, he excuses his own inability to address the task at hand. There's a reason we don't write organum any more: We know better.

THE MODERN MISTAKE

Those who fail to learn the lessons of history are doomed to repeat them.
George Santayana

Modernists failed to learn the Ars Nova's lesson.

The closest thing to an historical precedent for the modernist movement is the 14th Century *Ars Nova*. During that time, composers tried some fairly radical revisions to musical language—most notably, the isorhythmic motet, in which they systematically superimposed repetitive rhythmic patterns on repetitive melodic patterns of different lengths. It resembles the approach of the serialists in that its practitioners attempted to construct music by employing generative mathematical formulae. Like the modernist movement, it was misguided because its impetus was in the verbal-analytical mode. The *Ars Nova's* historical lesson is fairly simple: While it briefly raised some intriguing questions, it had very little impact on music's long-term development. Such pieces are trotted out as historical curiosities from time to time, but they can't be characterized as "speaking to us across the ages." Eventually, this will prove true for most modernist music as well—particularly that which relies heavily upon rigid non-intuitive systems.

Some modernists have, in fact, invoked the 14th Century *Ars Nova* as justification for verbal-analytical complexity in modern musical composition. For example, the following is from Charles Wuorinen's article, "Notes on Performance of Contemporary Music":

With respect to the supposed rhythmic difficulties of contemporary music (the area most often cited as the seat of unsolvable performance problems), two examples from the past seem relevant. Both have certain similarities to modern music; having participated in performances of both of them, I can attest that their demands are no less formidable than any made today. The first, part of *Le Greygnour Bien* of Matheus de Perusio (c. 1400), is hard enough to realize accurately when written in "modern" score form with all values referable to a bar line. But, when one considers the analog in modern notation of this example as written in the late 14th century, and further considers that there was no score, it becomes clear that the capacities of the Avignon musicians who performed it were in no way inferior to our own. (Incidentally, the musicological conceit—that this music, because of its "complexity," is "decadent"—is based on the premise that the symmetries of music of the recent past constitute a norm against which everything else, old and new, is to be measured. This premise, among other things, assumes that periodicity, exact durational and articulative symmetry, and binary division of duration are "basic"—an assumption not only contrary to fact and logically unacceptable but also belied by its difficulty of realization in practice: if these divisions were basic, why would beginning students, and many professionals, find such particular difficulty in playing "even" note values?)[23]

The history lesson that modernists ignored was this: The *Ars Nova* penchant for hidden meanings and rhythmic obfuscation didn't last. And, as the progress paradigm should illustrate, the demise of their approach to composition was no accident. It wasn't mere rhythmic complexity that caused it to fail. Chopin used complex cross rhythms quite effectively. And one would hardly argue that the rhythms in Stravinsky's *Rite of Spring* are simple. But *Ars Nova* composers, like many modernists, failed to establish a stable context for predicting complex structures over time. Consequently, listeners couldn't vicariously participate in the act of composition. My bet is that non-metrical rhythmic structure was "the seat of unsolvable performance problems" for 14th Century musicians as well. In

defense of the *Ars Nova* composers, polyphony itself was still a novel concept. It afforded a new level of communicability in that several messages
could be transmitted simultaneously, but composers still lacked principles
governing the coordination of the various parts. Their task of organizing
relationships among several simultaneous lines was further impeded
because they hadn't yet invented the musical score.

When Wuorinen cited the inability of students to play evenly, he didn't
successfully refute the natural superiority of evenness. Rather, he pointed
out the rhythmic awkwardness that many young students experience. A
student who has difficulty performing steady 8th notes would have far
greater difficulty with the following excerpt from Matheus de Perusio's *Le
Greygnour Bien*:

Wuorinen's statement was simply a rationalization. He used a previous
period's verbal-analytical mistake as the precedent for legitimizing the
modernists' verbal-analytical mistake. Folk music everywhere exhibits a
preference for steady note values. Even African drum music, which is
often cited as justification for modern rhythmic practices, generally consists of several players whose individual contributions are straightforward
and repetitive. It's only the cumulative effect that is complex. Wuorinen
was also wrong to suggest that the symmetries of music from the recent
past aren't norms against which music in general should be measured.
Psychological research confirms that audible symmetries are critical for

recognizing, storing, and retrieving significant patterns and that, in the absence of such patterns, meaning is lost.

Wuorinen's own 1970 Pulitzer Prize winning work, *Time's Encomium*, is fraught with similar flaws. In it, he introduces many colorful electronic sounds, but the piece fails to cohere because very little of it resembles biological rhythm and it provides almost no predictive assistance to the listener. Consequently, the audience is relegated to the sensuous plane, deprived of the ability to vicariously participate in the act of composition.

Modernists failed to properly define music.

According to the modernists, the universe was completely knowable and logical and it was our manifest destiny to decipher all of Nature's secrets and create a technology-based Utopia. When composers adopted the modernist mindset, they speculated about the future of music in ways that ostensibly resembled scientific inquiry. Realizing that the masterpieces of music history were elegantly structured, the modernists developed similarly elegant mathematical approaches to composition. Their systems were, indeed, highly ordered, clever, and rational. But, on the whole, they failed to write convincing works of music. This came about in large part because modernist composers neglected to begin by properly defining music—an odd mistake, considering their otherwise overtly intellectual approach. Musical order is of a very specific kind and its closest relatives in science are biology and psychology, not mathematics and physics—a fact that mysteriously eluded the modernists.

But the acknowledged masters of the past also wrote music without bothering to define it. Why did they succeed where the modernists failed? Why should it suddenly have become necessary to define something that has thrived for so long without benefit of a formal definition? The answer is fairly simple: Our ancestors hadn't attempted quite so radical a break with tradition. The process of learning craft from the elders and then contributing to the ongoing discourse naturally facilitated gradual but effective progress, so the musical fundamentals weren't seriously called into question. The modernists, however, tried to invent completely new systems of writing music—systems that intentionally disregarded fundamental aspects of traditional composition. In a sense, they tried to reinvent the language of music without first determining what its message was.

Serialist composer Milton Babbitt mentioned music's definition when he said, "To proceed from an assertion of what music has been to an assertion of what music, therefore, must be, is to commit a familiar fallacy." But it's not a fallacy—familiar or otherwise—to expect a word to retain its definition over time. If "air" refers to the stuff we breathe today, will it instead refer to a species of plant tomorrow? The exact content of air varies from time to time and from place to place, just as style varies from composer to composer, from continent to continent, and from period to period, but air remains air and music remains music. While its superficial characteristics obviously do vary, music must have an underlying set of definitive elements. Otherwise, the word means nothing.

Lacking a definition, modernists also lacked direction.

The end of the Romantic Era brought with it the collapse of common practice tonality. Left without a securely defined path, composers set out on individual quests for the elusive new voice. The pioneers of new periods had never before faced quite so daunting a task. This precipitated an extreme style consciousness that is uncharacteristic of previous period boundaries. Unfortunately, the absence of a valid definition of music precluded any objective method for evaluating the potential efficacy of a given approach to composition. As a consequence, many individuals "threw out the baby with the bath water" and failed to recover it upon subsequent reflection.

Modernists overemphasized novelty.

The 20th Century was unique in western music history in that it did not have a single handy label or a clear set of common characteristics. Several new and radically different styles emerged more or less at once. Many composers were searching for *the* new style, but no consensus was forthcoming. Since the objective was to find an entirely new approach to composition rather than to acquire the skills of the past masters and make a few course adjustments, novelty received undue emphasis. The new route to fame and fortune was through novelty—even in the absence of artistry.

The 20th Century brought many conspicuous advances in science. Composers began to model their quest for the elusive new style after the work of contemporary scientists. In fact, many modernist composers were actually educated as mathematicians, physicists, and engineers rather than musicians. A scientist gains recognition through *discovery*—by being the *first* to report something. Many composers sought and received recognition in a similar way. Being the first to use a new technique greatly enhanced one's chances of winning major awards, securing performances and recordings, and being assigned prestigious teaching posts. Extramusical factors like the academic composer's need to be published in order to achieve tenure began to exert pressure on the process of composition.

Scientists raced to find the building blocks of matter and of life, the origin of the universe, new sources of fuel, new medicines, and so forth. Composers raced to use new technology and to find the new techniques that would replace common practice. It was a period of brainstorming; any idea, however ridiculous, was valid. The most important thing was being *first* to use it. A "discovery" afforded someone the opportunity to publish articles in jargon-laden music theory journals like *Perspectives of New Music*. A musically unproven composer could be catapulted into a position of power and prestige by demonstrating his skill as a writer and analyst. Practitioners posited a plethora of pseudo-scientific concepts. Why choose the notes yourself when you can program a computer to do it for you? Why not choose the notes randomly—by rolling dice, for example?

Later modernists created ineffective systems.

Arnold Schoenberg proposed and demonstrated his serial technique—an alternative way of choosing notes in a composition. His approach possessed a certain mathematical elegance—an appealing characteristic that led other composers to elaborate. Why not apply the principle of serialism to other aspects of a piece? Why struggle over decisions about dynamics, phrasing, and articulation when you can parameterize these systematically and use an algorithm to generate them? This is the principle underlying *total serialism*. This idea and others like it led to articles teeming with intimidating techno-babble. Consider the following tidbit by Milton Babbitt, for example:

> The hexachordal inversional property can be expressed: $H_0 + T_t IH_0 = A$, for some t (1.1) where H signifies "hexachord," and the subscript to H denotes the order number associated with the first element of this hexachord (thus, for simplicity, an ordering of the H is assumed, but the property is independent of the particular ordering); I signifies the inversion operator (permutation), and T the transposition operator, with subscript t denoting the transposition number, which—for this type of combinatoriality—can assume any odd integral value; where the T operator is omitted, it is understood that t = 0. The + sign is used in the sense of set union, and $\cdot$ in the sense of set intersection. The members of the "sets" (hexachord, in this case) are pitch classes; A signifies "aggregate," which—for the moment—may be taken to mean any collection of 12 different pitch classes. It must be recalled that the I and T operators do not commute (or, alternatively, commute only to within complementation mod. 12), and—therefore—the indicated

order of operations is significant, and is to be read from right to left; the R and I, R and T, and T operators do commute.

Given a t that satisfies (1.1), then from that stated property, the following follow immediately, any one of which could serve equally well as the definition of this type of combinatoriality: $H_0 \cdot T_t I H_0 = \emptyset$ (the empty set); $H_0 + T_t R I H_6 = A$; $H_0 \cdot T_t R I H_6 = \emptyset$; $H_0 \cdot T_t I H_6 = H_0 + T_t I H_6$, etc., etc. by virtue of the rules of formation and transformation of the system itself. (It is necessary to remember that any twelve-tone set possesses the combinatorial attribute that S_{0-n} (the first n order numbers of a set) + $RS_{(n+1)-11} = A$.)[24]

I'm not challenging Babbitt's math, mind you. I trust that it's airtight. He was a math major, after all. My contention is that the entire exercise is pointless because set theory dwells properly in the domain of mathematics rather than music. Schoenberg originally proposed the 12-tone method in part because it possessed a high degree of order, as did traditional harmony. One of the hallmarks of past masterpieces is structural elegance. In many pieces, every note was so precisely suited to its context that no other note could properly be substituted. Schoenberg was searching for a new method of choosing notes that would afford similar elegance. It was a valiant effort. I don't want to minimize its importance. But, in the wrong hands, Schoenberg's approach was misinterpreted.

Schoenberg, who was a consummate composer, didn't intend to abandon musicality for the sake of structure. Rather, he intended to provide an alternative *method* of choosing notes, but less musically gifted followers attempted to build elaborate and rigid *systems* from it—shifting the emphasis from musical efficacy to mathematical rigidity. Such processes shift the responsibility for musical judgment from the composer's ear to a set of algorithms. Systematic approaches to composition can, indeed, produce elegant structures, but they are not likely to be *musical* structures. Even if a systematic approach is tentatively applied, the composer's choices *must* be tempered by aural sensitivity. What we discover upon reflection is that the *musical ear*—primarily a function of the pattern-recognizing and pattern-generating intuitive mode—*does* inform our choices with order—order that is as impressive as any that can be imposed by mathematical formulae and which is decidedly more musical.

Modernism led to undue emphasis on literary war-horses.

The musical *avant-garde* made an unprecedented leap from the fringe to the foreground during the last century. Undue pressure for novelty—as opposed to craft—was brought to bear upon academic composers; being the first to use a new technique was seen as akin to making a scientific discovery. But the resulting works were often decidedly unsatisfying for listeners—even for very musically sophisticated listeners. As *avant-garde* works proliferated, audiences began avoiding concerts that included them. Consequently, performers began eliminating them from programs. And so the performance of new literary music was relegated to academic settings. The void in public concerts was filled by repeated performances of the war-horses—the acknowledged masterpieces of European music from the 18th and 19th centuries. Gradually, the absence of new literature came to be accepted and, finally, to be expected. Now the war-horse tradition is the *status quo*. Performers are now trained with the expectation that they will go out into the world and perpetuate it.

Serialism offered no musical advantage.

There are two fronts on which a musical innovation might show progress. These are communicability and dramatic shape. Early serial works were significantly less communicative than the works of the Romantic Era and produced no advantage in dramatic shape. To demonstrate, I'll present the first several measures of Anton Webern's *Drei Gesänge, Op. 23*. Below are the basic materials he used for constructing this passage. The untransposed prime series (P0) consists of the twelve notes of the chromatic scale ordered as they appear on the upper left line below reading from left to right. The untransposed retrograde (R0) is the same set of notes read from right to left. The untransposed inversion (I0) appears on the upper right line and the untransposed retrograde inversion (RI0) is the same set reading from right to left. P6 and R6 (lower left) are the prime and retrograde series transposed up 6 half steps. I6 and RI6 (lower right) are the corresponding inversion and retrograde inversion:

Below are the first six measures of the piece. I've placed labels and brackets on the excerpt in order to facilitate discussion. The voice sings P0 intact and then begins R6. The piano accompaniment is constructed from R6 followed by RI6, P6 (starting on B—shared with the voice), R0, and begins I0 (starting on F—shared with the preceding R0).

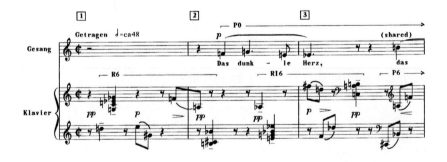

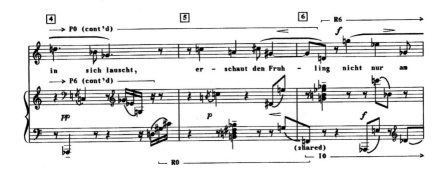

The voice part is chunked in accordance with the text. The first two phrases sung are also chunked in congruence with the meter (highest note of each is on a beat) and they share melodic contour. So, although the exact pitches of the second phrase can't be predicted based on the contents of the first phrase, the second phrase does provide sufficient logic to justify its presence upon reflection. The third and fourth phrases share syncopated quarter notes, so they contribute to a reasonably consistent effect, but there is still no audible cue for predicting pitches. The crescendo to forte in measure 6 places greatest emphasis on the highest note of the passage and the overall melodic structure does have a hierarchical dramatic shape.

The audible structure in the piano part is much more limited. From the outset Webern continuously avoids placing stress on beats that would establish an aural sense of meter. Although quarters and eighths are fairly consistently used, the intervals vary so that no pitch predictions can arise based on familiarity. The chords that are struck provide minimal textural consistency. But the placement of these chords offers almost no aural cues for prediction and no hierarchical reference. The first two statements of the series in the piano part (R6 followed by RI6) offer grouping consistency (single quarter note + 4-pitched chord + 2 pairs of slurred eighths + 3-pitched chord in each statement). Because RI6 is R6 inverted, the 4-pitch chord in measure 2 is the inversion of the 4-pitch chord in measure 1 (The first is a diminished triad with added fourth below and the second is a diminished triad with added fourth above) and so forth. But the audibility of these relationships is tenuous at best and they're placed inconsistently relative to the meter, so that grouping by familiarity is almost certain to fail. The brief flurry of sixteenths in measure 4 provides a bit of complementary motion—clearly delineating it from its surroundings by onset asynchrony and lack of common fate, but it isn't subsequently reinforced so it offers no predictive information. Individual pairs of eighths are weakly grouped by proximity and share some similarity where they occur (e.g., they all move by fairly large intervals and they're all slurred), but there's no audible basis for predicting when they'll occur or what their specific pitches will be. Consequently, the listener is deprived of the ability to vicariously participate in the act of composition. When expectations cannot be established, variations cannot be perceived as such. Consequently, delays aren't delays, so the law of affect doesn't apply. The dynamics in the piano part correspond with those in the voice part, including the crescendo to forte in measure 6. And the highest piano note nearly coincides with the highest voice note, so the accompaniment does show some evidence of support for a hierarchical dramatic shape. The piano part's metrical ambiguity actually detracts from the tension of the sung syncopations (Syncopation creates tension by displacing accents from the metrical frame of reference, but if the meter is uncertain the audience isn't sure where to *expect* accents, so placement seems arbitrary and displacement becomes insignificant).

Like the *Ars Nova's* isorhythms, serial technique imparted an overall consistency to texture but made moment-by-moment aural predictions extremely difficult—probably impossible. In fact, one of the aims of serialism was to avoid the very techniques that make structure audible. Schoenberg and his disciples set out to develop an entirely new language—one that would provide a new grammar, not just for choosing pitches but also for structuring phrases. In the process, they violated the Gestalt principles upon which traditional phrase structures were based. It was a noble effort, but it should have been regarded as a failed experiment and abandoned. Later modernists, lacking sufficiently elegant alternatives, adopted serialism as though it had proven its effectiveness and doggedly pressed ahead, often building serial structures that were considerably less audible than Schoenberg's.

Aleatory composers also failed to define music.

When scientists began to challenge the idea that the Universe was rigidly ordered according to a highly rational system of laws, some composers came to believe that music's structure was somehow artificially imposed—that it wasn't sufficiently random to reflect the emerging concept of nature. This, too, was because they neglected to define music. Despite all of the praise that was lavished upon John Cage for his use of randomization, the result of this process is chaotic. It deprives the listener of vicarious participation in the act of composition. I've heard it said that although Cage isn't much of a composer he is an important musical philosopher. How so? An important philosopher illuminates our way. The only lesson Cage offers is, "Don't do what I have done."

Music doesn't depict the fundamental nature of the Universe. It expresses biological rhythm as we humans experience it. Regardless of the complexity of the underlying physical principles, biological systems are self-ordering, as is human perception.

Although aleatory composers randomized the note selection process and serial composers applied systematic rules for note selection, the products often sounded remarkably similar. The reason is simple: For the purposes of human cognition, both approaches are essentially random because they supply little or no audible framework for recognizing relationships among the various textural components. There are ways to ameliorate this problem—at least in serial music—by constructing a series that's fraught with unambiguous tonal implications, by establishing audible order through elements other than pitch, and so forth. Returning intuition to its role is a crucial component to any solution, however. The verbal-analytical mode is probably incapable of competing with the pattern-searching intuitive mode when it comes to the development of new musical techniques. We'd be well advised to avoid theory-before-practice and simply analyze and admire what our intuitive modes generate. In any event, the proof is in the pudding. If a work is demonstrably less effective at representing biological rhythm or communicating with an audience than music from the late 19th and early 20th Centuries, then it represents a step backward for the progress paradigm.

Special effects composers misunderstood their predecessors.

However startling Igor Stravinsky's orchestration might seem, he actually continued more or less in the tradition of Berlioz, Tchaikovsky, and Rimsky-Korsakov. Later modernists mistook his use of effect and color as a cue to make the means into the end. Some modern works contain stunning successions of effects. Works that rely heavily upon effect generally have rather definite dramatic shape—owing to strong contrasts between the dynamic levels and textural densities of the various effects employed. But they also often lack audible clues by which listeners can predict the moment-by-moment progress of the piece. Consequently, the listening process is relegated to what Copland called the "sensuous plane" because there is no means for vicarious participation in the composition process.

Hector Berlioz said, "It [instrumentation] has...also served only too often to mask the poverty of a composer's ideas, to ape real energy, to counterfeit the power of inspiration, and even in the hands of really able and meritorious writers it has become a pretext for incalculable abuses, monstrous exaggerations, and ridiculous nonsense."[25] Arnold Schoenberg mirrored this sentiment when he said, "Perhaps the art of orchestration has become too popular, and interesting-sounding pieces are often produced for no better reason than that which dictates the making of typewriters and fountain pens in different colors."[26]

Orchestration serves to illuminate the architecture of a piece. It applies Gestalt principles like grouping by similarity in order to aurally segregate the texture's components. It also places special emphasis on the most significant patterns. The use of special effects without regard to audible cues for listeners can be quite effective in film music, where the purpose is accompaniment and the meaning—the significant pattern—lies in the dialog and action, but in concert halls, the music is the message. Consequently, emphasis on effects at the expense of significant audible patterns is a mistake.

Modernism set the stage for postmodernism.

By depriving audiences of the ability to participate vicariously in the composition process, the modernists disengaged listeners. As a result, the modernist movement precipitated the shift toward war-horse programming. That, in turn, fueled the postmodern notion that concert music represented only the work of dead white European males—that it was fundamentally sexist and racist. Although untrue, this assertion is difficult to counter because dead white European males did, indeed, write most of the music that is now played in our concert halls. Despite the fact that people of both genders and of all races and ethnic persuasions are now writing concert music, the music of dead white European males still dominates (on the order of 90%).

Concert music by living Americans is seldom performed.

A survey report on the American Symphony Orchestra League's web site regarding the 2001-2002 concert season repertoire may help to illuminate the magnitude of the problem—although that wasn't the report's intention. The top 10 scheduled composers were Beethoven (556 performances); Mozart (540); Brahms (394); Tchaikovsky (321); Richard Strauss (262); Mahler (227); Ravel (204); Haydn (203); Shostakovich (187); Prokofiev (183). The top 10 U.S. or Canadian composers were Barber (133); Bernstein (101); Copland (66); Adams (52); Gershwin (47); Hindemith (43); Rouse (42); Walton (34); Schwantner (33); Rautavaara (32).

The top 10 composers listed were all dead Europeans. Their works were performed five times as often as those of the top 10 American/Canadian composers. Samuel Barber—the *first* of the top 10 Americans—received 50 fewer performances than Prokofiev—the *last* of the top 10 dead Europeans. Four of the top five American/Canadian composers are dead—Barber (d. 1981); Bernstein (d. 1990); Copland (d. 1990); Gershwin (d. 1937). Three of the top 10 American/Canadian composers aren't even American or Canadian. Hindemith is a dead German. Walton is a dead Englishman. Rautavaara is a living Fin. Only three of the top 10 American/Canadian composers are living Americans (Adams, Rouse, and Schwantner) and none are Canadian.

Most of the music performed was written over 100 years ago. Of the remainder, most was written by Europeans who died before the end of the 20th Century. The top 10 pieces performed were all by dead Europeans. They ranged from 39 performances (Debussy's *La Mer*) to 53 performances (Tchaikovsky's *6th Symphony*). The average number of performances per work (3,432 / 1,737) is roughly two. Many of the dead European works had staggeringly high numbers of performances while the Americans averaged fewer than two performances each—and probably only slightly more than one.

There were 83 world premieres scheduled—mostly works by Americans who are not so well known as the top 10. Most received exactly one performance. Many weren't broadcast. Some probably weren't even recorded or reviewed. Most will not be released on commercial CDs. I point this out because major orchestras around the globe have recorded virtually all of the music written by famous dead Europeans—in many cases on dozens of different labels. And it has been broadcast thousands of times—also around the globe. Nearly everybody in the civilized world can hear any Brahms orchestral work simply by going to the classical record section of a store or library. But the only people who have heard or will ever hear those new American pieces are the people who attended those performances. It's not that they'll be discarded because they're bad pieces. They'll be shelved even if they're *great*.

They just won't be reviewed or recorded or scheduled elsewhere because there are so few opportunities afforded to new American music.

The average length of the pieces by the dead Europeans programmed was probably over 20 minutes and possibly over 30. There were shorter works, of course, but there were also hundreds of performances of extended works by Bruckner, Mahler, Shostakovich, and others. The average duration of new American works that actually get performed is under 10 minutes and probably closer to five. The bottom line is that fewer than 10% of the titles performed were by living Americans and less than 5%—probably less than 3%—of actual performance time in American orchestras was devoted to music by living Americans.

Historically, concert music audiences expected to hear new and challenging literature. Concerts that included world premieres were quite fashionable until around the middle of the 20th Century. The current tactic of performing 18th and 19th Century literary war-horses is unprecedented and it has failed in part because recorded versions of these works are abundantly available and in part because the war-horses are beginning to lose their relevance. The war-horse approach has turned our concert halls into museums. It has led directly to the "graying" of the American concert music audience. The average age of a symphony audience member is now about 68. Even as this graying threatens to become the dying, the trend persists—despite evidence that younger and larger audiences can be attracted to concerts that offer something new.

The war-horse-museum mentality was adopted because playing modernist music threatened to reduce audience size. Desperate to attract younger audiences, orchestras started performing more and more "pops" concerts. Ostensibly, the "pops" rationale was that it would attract the public to concert halls with familiar music and eventually the more curious and adventuresome listeners would be enticed to attend serious concerts as well—a sort of "bait and switch" scheme. This notion might seem appealing, but it has failed miserably. Many non-musicians simply came to perceive Broadway medleys and film scores as the new "classical" literature. The unfortunate fact that "pops" concerts are presented by highly trained and acclaimed musicians validates this view. The "pops" failure is that it actually discourages people from bothering to cultivate their listening skills. If they can already understand and enjoy "pops" music, which is apparently important literature, then wrestling with the difficult task of understanding the more "serious" fare is perceived as unnecessary.

The war-horse and "pops" phenomena helped to fuel the postmodern argument that all attempts at qualitative judgment in the arts are culturally biased. The war-horse approach led to cries of sexism and racism (because white males wrote all of the war-horses) and "pops" concerts supported the claim that popular music is artistically just as valid as literary music. Furthermore, the modernist propensity for wide-ranging "brainstorming" and novelty over substance abetted the postmodern assertion that "anything goes."

Though flawed, modernism contributed to the discourse.

During the 20th Century, we witnessed some novel and interesting experiments that, although they may have failed musically, were intellectually stimulating. They gave us pause. The developments of the period challenged our thinking and broadened our perspectives regarding resources that might be used in musical composition, so the ultimate impact has had some value. But the greatest lesson we can learn from the mid-20th Century's vast experimentation is that intuition is the final authority in music, not the verbal-analytical mode.

Many people have claimed that the modernists were "too cerebral," but that was not true. Bach, Mozart, Beethoven, and Brahms were all cerebral composers. They all wrote music that exhibits extraordinarily elegant order. However, they didn't place systematic approaches to composition above musicality; indeed, the cerebral aspect of their writing was specifically directed *toward* musicality. The modernists' "cerebral" problem was that they often wrote music in which fundamental constructs were born in the verbal-analytical mode and justified in extramusical terms. It wasn't the "smartness" of the modernists' music that made so much of it ineffective. Rather, it was the misdirection of their intellectual efforts.

We should not be too surprised by the modernists' failures. Reactionary points in music history involve composers whose contributions are more in the realm of struggling with new concepts than with writing major masterpieces. This kind of unsung groundwork is essential to the long-term evolution of concert music. But it's time to begin scrutinizing the efficacy of new methods as they relate to recent findings in the study of human perception. The early modernists provided us with some nuggets worth investigating further—polytonality and pantonality, shifting meters, striking orchestral colors, modes and alternative scales, quartal harmony, extended chords, harmonic successions without common practice implications, and so forth. But a great deal of the modernist music from the middle of the 20th Century gave us sediment.

It is likely that my discussion of modernism will be misinterpreted—possibly *intentionally* for political reasons—so I want to make it quite clear that it is possible to write effective music using many of the modernist techniques. What the various psychological principles tell is, however, that audibility should not be sacrificed for the sake of a system. Regardless of style, effective music facilitates storage in memory and provides audible clues about relationships among its various components.

POSTMODERN CULTURE

*That men do not learn very much from the lessons of history
is the most important of all the lessons of history.*
Aldous Huxley

Postmodernism is the prevalent pseudo-philosophical doctrine of our time. Because it is so pervasive, it's hard to explain what's wrong with postmodern music without addressing some of the larger aspects of the problem. Superficially, postmodernism seems quite accommodating. Some aspects of it arise from good intentions, but at its core is a fundamental assault on intellectual integrity. The term is applied rather broadly and loosely in various fields. If you ask a postmodernist what the movement is, he'll likely respond with a trite witticism like, "You're soaking in it." It's somewhat difficult to define because it's more of an *attitude* than a reasoned philosophical position, but its proponents generally claim that it includes the following attributes:

- *denial of objective knowledge*
- *equality among ideas—even contradictory ones*
- *equality among cultures (multiculturalism)*
- *alternative ways of knowing*
- *increased self-awareness*
- *denial of progress*
- *emphasis on values*

In theory, postmodernism represents heightened self-awareness, sensitivity, and equality. In practice, however, this noble-sounding agenda is characterized by excessive consumption, exaltation of mediocrity, desensitization, abrogation of responsibility, reduced civility, shallow thinking, and censorship. On the one hand, it conjures up a vision of world peace—a vision for which it offers no plan. On the other hand, it undermines the rule of law upon which peace depends.

Postmodernism relies on the objectivity it claims to refute.

One of the pillars of postmodernist writings is the notion that we cannot directly access objective reality and, consequently, we cannot discover an absolute truth (Truth with a capital "T"). Radical postmodernists assert that the physical world doesn't exist at all while less radical postmodernists merely claim that we can't *prove* anything about the physical world. According to the dogma, all opinion is culturally biased, so there can be no objective basis for determining what is right or wrong, good or bad, true or false. This proposition *("I know that I can't know anything")* is, in fact, self-contradictory. Logically, its proponents cannot assert that it is true without first acknowledging that truth exists.

In the scientific community, theories are considered tentative in the sense that they are subject to review and may be revised or rejected based upon conflicting evidence. However, postmodernist writers have misconstrued the meaning of "tentative" by claiming that there is little or no relationship between scientific inquiry and objective reality. They interpret differences between informed and uninformed opinions as mere conflicts of cultural bias.

Our access to the world of objects is non-verbal. If you put your hand on a hot stove burner, you'll withdraw it almost instantly—long before the word "hot" can formulate in your mind. If you see someone familiar, you may struggle to recall her name, even though you immediately recognize her face. Despite the difficulties in verbalizing our relationship to the external world, the outright denial of our connection with it is ridiculous. But postmodern writers work with language, which is largely confined to the verbal-analytical mode, and which is far removed from our more direct apprehension of sensory input. They often glean superficial information from philosophic or scientific sources and then distort the original meanings in order to "support" wild conclusions. But to deny our access to objective reality is to deny the very tools that postmodern writers use to propagate their agenda. They set their words on real paper for publication in real books that people buy in real bookstores.

The first fact is that existence exists. It is self-evident. It requires no verbal-analytical support. It's more compelling than any verbal argument. Although philosophers have posited some intriguing alternatives (e.g., the world exists only as my dream or an evil demon controls what I perceive), such alternatives are not at all compelling. We all—postmodern writers included—rely upon physical facts in order to survive and function. There are no rational alternatives. Suppose a bespectacled youngster on a school playground encounters a bully who says, "I'm going to beat you up, break your glasses, and steal your lunch money." The youngster responds with, "Oh yeah? Prove it." What ensues is not an erudite epistemological discourse. It's a thrashing, a pair of broken glasses, and stolen lunch money. It's proof that transcends mere language.

Our senses don't present the world to us as a complex system of interacting particles and waves (a fact that postmodernist writers twist to their advantage). Instead, they provide "shorthand"—just enough to facilitate our survival. Nonetheless, assuming that our nervous systems develop normally, we can directly (if imperfectly) observe physical objects in our world.

Conceptualization proceeds from the non-verbal and concrete to the verbal and abstract, not *vice versa*. Early forays into mathematics, for example, rely upon physical "props." A parent or teacher presents an object and recites a number along with the object's name ("one apple"), then increases the number ("two apples"). The abstract concept of counting eventually takes root in the child's mind, because it has been reinforced by the world of objects. Eventually, concepts of addition and subtraction are undertaken by physical demonstration (one apple + one apple = two apples). Later, the apples can be hypothetical ("If I had two apples and I gave you one, how many apples would I have left?"). But such concepts lag far behind the associated physical perceptions themselves.

Before red and green, big and small, fuzzy and smooth, wet and dry, hard and soft, and hot and cold can be conceptualized and cataloged, they must be experienced. Imagine trying to explain "red" to a blind person or "high pitched" to a deaf person. No matter how carefully you choose the words, the concept will elude your audience. It is the direct experience of redness and highness that inform your concepts about them.

Once you conceptualize redness, you can recognize it when you see unfamiliar red objects in your environment. And other people who recognize red when they see it will concur that the objects you call red are the ones they call red. If we apply Ockham's Razor, we discover that the most reasonable explanation for this phenomenon—indeed, the *only* reasonable explanation—is that the objects we call red are, in fact, red. And, if redness exists in the physical world, then we should be able to detect it and measure it with physical instruments. Enter the spectroscope. It doesn't conceptualize; it just detects and measures light waves. So it confirms that our experience of redness does, indeed, correspond to reflective properties of objects in the physical world.

Postmodernists often invoke cutting-edge research to support their claim that we can't discover objective truth—that scientific inquiry itself is an entirely subjective process. But the fact that objective reality has some counterintuitive aspects does not mean that it is fundamentally undecipherable. Furthermore, if there were no connection between scientific inquiry and objective reality, then it would be illogical to cite scientific findings as evidence that the universe is unknowable. In his article, "The Sleep of Reason," Thomas Nagel refutes the postmodern claim that science cannot be objective:

> Much of what Kuhn says about great theoretical shifts, and the inertial role of long-established scientific paradigms and their cultural

entrenchment in resisting recalcitrant evidence until it becomes over-whelming, is entirely reasonable, but it is also entirely compatible with the conception of science as seeking, and sometimes finding, objective truth about the world. What has made him a relativist hero is the addi-tion of provocative remarks to the effect that Newton and Einstein, or Ptolemy and Galileo, live in "different worlds," that the paradigms of different scientific periods are "incommensurable," and that it is a mis-take to think of the progress of science over time as bringing us closer to the truth about how the world really is.

Feyerabend is more consistently outrageous than Kuhn, deriding the privileged position of modern science as a way of understanding the world. "All methodologies have their limitations," he says in *Against Method*, "and the only 'rule' that survives is 'anything goes'." As Sokal and Bricmont point out, the first clause of this sentence may be true, but it does not in any way support the second.

Both [Kuhn and Feyerabend] are repeatedly cited in support of the claim that everything, including the physical world, is a social con-struct existing only from the perspective of this or that cognitive prac-tice, that there is no truth but only conformity or nonconformity to the discourse of this or that community, and that the adoption of sci-entific theories is to be explained sociologically rather than by the pro-bative weight of reasoning from the experimental evidence. Scientists don't believe this, but many nonscientists now do…Bruno Latour recently challenged as anachronistic the report of French scientists who examined the mummy of Ramses II that the pharaoh had died of tuberculosis, because the tuberculosis bacillus came into existence only when Robert Koch discovered it in 1882.

The postmodernist doctrine that there is nothing outside the text, no world to which it is tied down, seems plausible to the consumers of post-modernist writings because it is so often true of those writings, where lan-guage is simply allowed to take off on its own. Those who have no objective standards themselves find it easy to deny them to others…

Thus quantum theory, via the Heisenberg indeterminacy principle, and to a lesser extent relativity, are often invoked to show that today even science has had to abandon the idea of an objective, mind-independent reality. But neither theory has this significance, however strange may be the reality that they describe and its interaction with observers.[27]

Postmodernism promotes shallow thinking.

The postmodern *mantras* of "Who's to say?" and "Anything goes!" are closely allied with apathetic whines like "Who cares?" and "What's the difference?" They're intended to cut short a dialog when it becomes too complex for pat answers. The postmodern affirmation that all opinions are equal can be applied like a shield to deflect serious debate while ostensibly granting the speaker the moral high ground ("I'm magnanimous and you're not"). It's self-contradictory because it presumes its own *a priori* superiority ("The opinion that all opinions are equal is above reproach"). But it's not superior—morally or intellectually—to dodge a difficult topic by asserting that all opinions are equal when some are clearly inferior. It's just a cop-out.

Suppose you're arguing about an issue that you've studied thoroughly and about which you have an informed and carefully considered opinion. You're debating with somebody who hasn't studied the issue. He simply responds moment by moment with verbal "knee-jerks." Eventually, it becomes clear that you've reached an impasse. How do you bow out? You might say, "You're wrong, but you're entitled to your opinion." Or you might say, "I disagree with you but, of course, it's just a matter of opinion anyway."

The first exit line reflects the principle underlying the first amendment to the U.S. Constitution. Although your opponent's ignorant "knee-jerks" are inferior to your informed position, he has the right to express them. That's fine. The second statement suggests that the truth itself is relative— that it's just "a matter of opinion." The first statement exhibits tolerance;

the second, indifference. It may be non-confrontational, but it resolves nothing. Consequently, it promotes gridlock rather than action.

Postmodernism responds to modernist shortcomings.

One common postmodern claim is that progress is an illusion. Modern science, which promised us a futuristic Utopia, has instead proven to be a mixed bag. Science has given us pesticides but also resistant pests; nuclear power plants but also nuclear weapons and waste; cars, highways, and public utilities but also environmental damage; amazing medical technology but also accelerated overpopulation, and so forth. Science has vastly expanded our knowledge but we've been imprudent in applying it. Postmodernism represents, in large part, a "knee-jerk" reaction blaming scientific and technological progress for many of society's failures. But the denial of progress is shortsighted. For the first several hundred thousand years of human existence, the average life expectancy was about 18 years. The shift from hunter-gatherer to agrarian to industrial societies increased the human life span dramatically. In 1900, the average U.S. life expectancy was 49. Thanks to tremendous advances in medical science, it's now about 76.

Over tens of thousands of years, our ancestors gradually improved their technology in order to survive and prosper. They knew that their ingenuity wasn't wasted. Although there have been many setbacks, the general direction of history has been forward—toward ever more sophisticated technology and improved living conditions. As new and useful tools are invented, they are implemented and propagated. In the process, Man has experienced very real progress. It would be difficult to argue that people were better off when they died before age 30 or that safe drinking water, public transportation systems, modern hospitals, and electrical appliances offer no benefits.

Postmodernists often cite the two World Wars as evidence that modernism has failed, but that claim is erroneous. War and genocide have been with us since the dawn of humanity. Basically it's only the weapons that have changed. And the vast scope of the World Wars was commensurate with our recent population increase and general globalization. I'm not trying to justify war; I'm just pointing out that it's not a product of modernism. Postmodernists also offer the World Wars as evidence that human society has not progressed socially, but I would argue that the modern world's emphasis on democracy and human rights has greatly improved the human condition—at least in the industrialized world.

Day-to-day life for the ancient peasant was considerably more brutal than it is for the average American citizen now. However, there are still parts of the world that are quite uncivilized—not because modernity has failed, but because it has not yet transformed the most hostile and irrational cultures. The simplistic postmodernists fail to appreciate the enormous obstacles that our forebears overcame in order to establish the rule of law and bestow civil rights on commoners, thereby making at least part of the world more civil.

The claim against progress also involves a significant element of hypocrisy. Postmodernists enjoy the technological and social benefits of living in the modern world while claiming that it is not objectively better than its alternatives. But how many postmodernists would willingly migrate to less modern societies—societies that are inhabited by the ignorant and ruled by the oppressive? The most conspicuous area of progress is in our knowledge of the world. Because postmodern writers deny the validity of that knowledge, they impede progress. Theirs is a self-fulfilling prophecy.

American postmodernism took root during the 1960's.

The rate of change in the modern world—arising largely from scientific and technological progress—is accelerating. Recent insights have challenged long-accepted notions about the world. As a result, many people in the World War II generation were left bewildered and many of the Baby Boomers (my generation) began asserting simplistic new answers to the questions that have been raised. Our parents were the children of the Great Depression. They fought and won a major global war. They experienced hardships that we have not. They invested heavily in the future of their children because they wanted us to have opportunities that were unavailable to them. Theirs was the optimistic attitude of the modernists.

The typical Boomer lived a childhood of plenty. That, unfortunately, allowed many of us to exaggerate minor hardships (like college attendance and grading policies, dorm curfews, visitation restrictions, and dress codes). Boomers completed high school and went on to college in record numbers. Some believed that people in our generation knew more than our less educated parents and that we should set the world aright by exposing the injustices of their world—the world of dominating white males and the military industrial complex. On the whole, the protest movement was a large-scale temper tantrum perpetrated by pampered adolescents. Its cadre of misguided elders—people like Timothy Leary ("turn on, tune in, and drop out")—were quick to find fault with the existing system but had no idea how to fix it. As Allan Bloom pointed out in *The Closing of the American Mind*, the righteous indignation of the 60's involved more than a little hypocrisy:

> A final part of the mythology of the sixties is the alleged superior moral "concern" of the students. Morality became all the rage in the late sixties, succeeding the hard-nosed realism of the preceding years. But what was meant by morality has to be made clear. There is a perennial and unobtrusive view that morality consists in such things as telling the truth, paying one's debts, respecting one's parents and doing no voluntary harm to anyone. Those are all things easy to say and hard to do; they do not attract much attention, and win little honor in the world. The good will, as described by Kant, is a humble notion, accessible to every child, but its fulfillment is the activity of a lifetime of performing the simple duties prescribed by it. This morality always requires sacrifice...This was not the morality that came into vogue in

the sixties, which was an altogether more histrionic version of moral conduct…Somehow it was never the everyday business of obeying the law that was interesting; more so was breaking it in the name of the higher law…

The slogan was "Make love, not war." Although the similarity of language was exploited, this is very different from "Love thy neighbor," which is an injunction very difficult to fulfill. To "make love" is a bodily act, very easy to perform…Moderation of the infinite bodily desires had become "repression" of nature, one of the forms of *domination*, the buzzword of the advanced thinkers and consciousness raisers. All that was needed were the heroes willing to act out the fantasies the public was now ready to accept as reality: the hero, as hedonist, who dares to do in public what the public wants to see…

A partial list of the sacrifices made by the students to their morality will suffice to show its character: they were able to live as they pleased in the university, as *in loco parentis* responsibilities were abandoned; drugs became a regular part of life, with almost no interference from university authorities, while the civil authority was kept at bay by the university's alleged right to police its own precincts; all sexual restrictions imposed by rule or disapproval were overturned; academic requirements were relaxed in every imaginable way, and grade inflation made it difficult to flunk; avoidance of military service was a way of life and a principle. All of these privileges were disguised with edifying labels such as individual responsibility, experience, growth, development, self-expression, liberation, concern. Never in history had there been such a marvelous correspondence between the good and the pleasant. Richard Nixon, with his unerring instinct for the high moral ground and the noble motive for consensus, assessed his student antagonists and ended the draft. Miraculously the student movement came to an end, although the war continued for almost three years thereafter.[28]

Some of the activists' issues did have merit (e.g., the movement to eliminate racial segregation). However, the students tacitly assumed that *all* of
their complaints were valid and that they were better able to judge the
merits of their cause than were the schools and government institutions
that stood in their way. The student position was one that would accept
no compromise, no negotiation. It was a movement of impatience and
belligerence and, occasionally, of violence. It often had little in common
with the ideal of world peace it was ostensibly intended to foster. Its leaders were more interested in the unrestricted availability of sex and drugs
than in making the world better.

Postmodernism has unwittingly made our society less civil.

The "Age of Aquarius" is nowhere in sight. The U.S. has less than 5% of the
world's human population but more than 30% of its prison population. Our
current crime rate statistics were undoubtedly difficult for "flower children"
to foresee, but their roots are, nonetheless, in the movement. The student
activists pushed aside the rule of law—not for the noble motives often
espoused, but for simple self-gratification. They didn't really understand the
laws or the historical context in which they were established. They didn't have
a carefully developed new plan to supersede the existing system. They just
broke laws because they didn't want to obey them.

Civilization is a fragile thing. It relies upon the rule of law and upon the
elders' ability to indoctrinate the youth. The student movement of the 60's
basically reversed this process, forcing the elders to adopt the values of the
young. By undermining parental and institutional authority, the Boomer
generation relinquished much of its own control over the next generation.
How can parents tell their children to "toe the line" when they did not?

The activists were thinking as children, not as parents—spoiled children at that. And they got their way: Kids are now less accountable for
their actions. When they do something wrong, the responsibility rests

with parents, schools, and "society at large," but not with them. And kids know it. Consequently, many of our schools are now war zones.

Selfishness has become a virtue. The easiest path has become the best. After all, in the absence of objective knowledge, who's to say otherwise? We've increased emphasis on our rights and decreased emphasis on our responsibilities. Someone who once would have been called "conscientious" is now "anal-retentive." Someone who once would have been "obnoxious" is now "assertive."

We've become a nation of litigation—much of it frivolous—aimed at windfall profits rather than justice. Once the land of opportunity, ours is now the land of opportunists. Accountability has shifted from individuals to larger institutions—also a carryover from the 60's, when every evil was the fault of "the establishment." People should be able to do as they wish and not be held accountable. Society at large is to blame when things go wrong. If students fail, it's because schools are inferior. If people die, it's because products are unsafe. If drunk drivers kill, it's because bartenders don't stop them from drinking. The main thing is that *somebody else* is responsible—preferably somebody with enough money to offer an attractive settlement.

Our icons are excessive and hedonistic—precisely what the 60's movement prescribed. The violent crime rate is at an all-time high. Even so, the number of rock and movie stars who've been convicted of violent crimes has soared disproportionately relative to the entire population. Why? Because we idolize their flagrant "heroic" excesses. Drug abuse has become the mark of "artistic temperament" instead of decadence. We treat rockers who die from overdoses like martyrs.

Postmodern multiculturalism is shortsighted.

The postmodern multicultural view, which asserts that all cultures are equal (meaning that nobody can judge the relative merits of a particular culture), purportedly extends to all cultures and religions. But blind acceptance that all cultures are equal undermines well-founded American convictions that all people should share certain fundamental rights and that rigid class structures, chauvinistic societies, military dictatorships, genocide, racial segregation, and religious oppression are unjust. Fortunately, in practice, postmodernists are properly irate about human rights abuses. Somehow, the conflict between the notion of equality among cultures and the goal of alleviating human suffering eludes them.

The argument for "alternative ways of knowing" is irrational.

During the 60's, students began a quest for new ways of looking at the world. If the primarily Christian, male-dominated society into which we were born was wrong, then perhaps better alternatives existed elsewhere. They turned to ancient Eastern religions, transcendental meditation, witchcraft, and so forth. They didn't find better answers to life's most perplexing questions, but many thought they had. "What's your sign?" became a popular pick-up line.

The concept of alternative ways of knowing is legitimate, so long as its meaning is limited to specifically knowable aspects of human behavior. For example, an athlete has an alternative way of calculating trajectory when he throws a ball ("muscle memory" rather than mathematics). An artist has an alternative way of understanding visual symbolism when she grasps the potentially multi-layered meanings of an image (e.g., the Golden Arches represent the letter "M" in McDonalds but also resemble Mommy's breasts—thus subliminally suggesting love, comfort, and security to unsuspecting kids).

Unfortunately, the postmodern concept of "alternative ways of knowing" embraces irrational behavior and dogmatic traditions. It lends credence to superstitious mumbo jumbo like telepathy, clairvoyance, and psychic healing. It also legitimizes drug abuse. Mysticism and superstition aren't alternative ways of knowing. They're alternative manifestations of ignorance and irrationality. LSD isn't a "mind-expanding" drug; it's a hallucinogen. It doesn't reveal an alternative reality. It doesn't improve one's intellect or heighten one's sensitivity or self-awareness. It just distorts moods, perceptions, and interpretations of the *real* reality. The bottom line is quite simple: If you want a reasonably accurate weather forecast, consult a meteorologist, not a psychic hotline.

Militant feminists employed revisionist history.

The righteous indignation of militant feminists during the 60's exhibited a very limited grasp of the world we had inherited. The "dominating white males" of America's past laid down their lives in revolt against a class structure based on birthrights in order to secure democracy and elevate the dignity of the commoner. Later, white men from the north fought and died to abolish slavery. Most of the men from my grandfather's generation and my father's generation fought in World Wars I and II—not because they were "war mongers," but because circumstances mandated it. When they came home, they worked under extremely difficult and often dangerous conditions to build our nation's infrastructure, to establish a strong economy and a responsive system to aid the old and disabled. These weren't "male chauvinist pigs." They were dedicated to achieving social justice, not domination. But progress was incremental. Once the necessities were assured, they turned to labor-saving devices for their wives—self-cleaning ovens, self-defrosting freezers, permanent press clothes, prepared foods, etc. The women of my father's generation knew enough about factory conditions that most of them didn't want their husbands' jobs. Many of them had first-hand experience in factories during World War II.

Most couples discussed how their homes and lives were managed, just as we do now. Housework was much more demanding than it is now, but most women didn't object to being housewives because they hadn't yet been taught that it was a demeaning occupation. In fact, it was no more demeaning than their husbands' backbreaking labor in coalmines and assembly lines, but it was *safer*. Working outside the home wasn't a privilege that was granted to men and denied to women. It was a duty. Men were *expected* to work in order to provide for their families, just as women were *expected* to nurture their children. On the whole, men tried to *protect* their wives and provide for their children, not to dominate them. Men served in the military out of a sense of duty, not because they wanted to deprive women of combat careers. There was still a bit of chivalry in the world, but feminists perverted its meaning. Why? Because the old chivalry included genuine moral values like duty and commitment—for men and women alike. It wasn't *selfish* enough for the new agenda. It became necessary to revise the past—to demonize white males.

The feminist claim that men chauvinistically kept women "barefoot, pregnant, and in the home" was conveniently timed. It coincided with improved factory conditions and an economic shift from production jobs to service jobs, making work outside the home significantly more attractive. But it was Nature that dictated the historic distribution of labor, not men. In 1956, Dr. Gregory Pincus invented the birth control pill. When the FDA approved it in 1960, it radically altered women's prospects. It was a victory of modern medicine over nature, not of women over men. Until then, the only effective means of avoiding pregnancy was abstinence. How could women have expected to bear unpredictable numbers of children while managing careers outside their homes?

Postmodernism fosters excessive consumerism.

Andy Warhol is a postmodern icon. His paintings of rows of matching Campbell's soup cans suggests a bit about what postmodernism really represents: mass production and its helpmate, mass consumption. Modern industry gave us the ability to make stuff—lots of stuff. Early in the 20th Century, modern factories supplied inexpensive goods that improved living conditions, health, and longevity. But as industry grew and became ever more efficient, production overtook consumption. Consequently, industry now invests in massive advertising campaigns to convince us that we need more stuff. Industry now plans obsolescence for the stuff we have.

Advertisers convince us that we need the latest stuff—the "new and improved" stuff. We need to discard perfectly serviceable clothing in order to buy this year's fashions. Popular music styles change with each decade so we need new CD collections. And we need bigger stuff. Bigger is better. We need bigger houses with Jacuzzis and swimming pools. Cars are OK for a start, but we also need SUVs, pick-up trucks, campers, RVs, boats, trailers, and jet skis. Wide-screen TVs aren't big enough; we need home theater systems. We need "super-sized" servings at fast food restaurants. Before "Cabbage Patch Kids," the prospect of deadly toy store stampedes would have seemed absurd. But now, people *must* have brand name products—ostensibly because they're better, but really because their manufacturers can earn higher profit margins and eliminate competitors. Kids are "out of style" if they don't have Nike "swishes" on their shoes.

The U.S. has become the spoiled child of the industrialized world. We have an extremely large global "footprint." Our country consumes about 1/3 of the resources used but has less than 5% of the world's population. And, thanks in part to "super-sizing," ours is now the fattest country on Earth. Nonetheless, thanks to the postmodern denial of objective truth, our politicians can claim that scientific reports about environmental damage "need further study" and that we should avoid committing to related international agreements (e.g., the Kyoto Accord) until the developing nations make similar concessions—even though they have nothing to give up. And the fact that our measure of economic health is tied to GDP growth exacerbates the problem.

Advertising drives this irrational consumption. Carefully constructed images redirect real human needs by telling uncritical consumers that if they buy the right products, they'll be sexier, they'll have good taste, they'll get promoted, they'll be loved, they'll show that they care. In reality, they'll just be deeper in debt. The relentless pursuit of that elusive "good life" now requires two breadwinners per household. The WW II generation's prudent admonition to avoid "keeping up with the Joneses" has been cast aside. The new message is, "BE the Joneses." You want it now. You're worth it. Just do it.

Buy it on credit. The answer to the postmodern question, "Who's to say?" is simple: Business.

Postmodernism is desensitizing.

Reality shows and trailer-trash-oriented talk shows have replaced more wholesome and intelligent fare because they boost ratings. In the absence of objective judgment, "anything goes." Most of the new heroes are either rock stars or movie stars. Many are self-centered hedonists specifically groomed for stardom because of their propensity for excess. It is precisely this quality that makes our adolescents admire them, worship them, imitate them, and—most important—lavish money on them. Ostensibly, they're exercising freedom of expression. In fact, they're fulfilling exactly the roles they've been assigned by the entertainment industry. They're not rebelling against the establishment. They *are* the establishment.

Many "blockbuster" special effects movies are also desensitizing. Instead of meaningful dialog, insightful character development, and original story lines, they offer loud, incessant rock sound tracks (geared toward record sales) and careful product placement (also geared toward sales). Dazzling special effects distract viewers from absurd plots. Their heroes often sneer out colorful, humorous, but insensitive catch phrases while brutally dispatching their enemies (handy "trailer" material for marketing the movies themselves): "Hasta la vista, baby!" These movies allow the Hollywood "suits" to do what they do best—count the money. There's a lot more than just ticket revenue to count, too. There are also movie-related dolls and action figures, comic books, tee shirts and underoos, lunchboxes, knapsacks, candies, cereals, video games, Halloween costumes, soundtrack albums, marketing campaigns coordinated with fast-food chains, and more.

In the absence of any other measure, the bottom line is the default measure of quality. The film industry makes movies, then lavishes praise on the movies that make money so they can escalate the hyperbole so they can create a market for sequels, prequels, spin-offs, and knock-offs. The entertainment industry gets publicity from the news media (largely owned by the industry) that present their hyperbole-laden awards ceremonies and pre-opening "blitzes" as news. And when the process is criticized, the industry responds with, "We're just giving the public what it wants."

What the industry strives to do (with great success) is to shape our expectations so that we conform to their marketing strategy. They don't give us what we want; they make us want what they give us. And the easiest path to success is to peddle their wares to unsuspecting, uncritical, unsophisticated adolescents, which is exactly what they do. In turn, our adolescents remain unexposed to more intelligent, mind-engaging forms of entertainment, so their thinking remains shallow. They become desensitized by loud soundtracks and ubiquitous special effects and, therefore, less likely to expect intelligent fare in the future. In short, our kids are being trained to be uncritical, mindless consumers. The industry's system is a self-perpetuating biofeedback loop of unprecedented scope. It has nothing to do with art and everything to do with commerce.

> It is a shame when people reject the best traditions and practices of the world's most talented artists in favor of music that is the most amateurish and least sophisticated. In few other areas of human activity do people reject the best and prefer the worst. Not many people would prefer to watch sporting events featuring the most poorly trained and least accomplished athletes, or buy clothes designed and crafted by amateurs in a folksy, homespun style; prefer that a complicated surgical procedure be performed by a self-taught physician, or trust their financial futures in a civil suit to an untrained "garage" attorney. Strangely, when it comes to music, it seems for some otherwise intelligent, educated adults, the cruder the better. Go figure.[29]

Postmodernism has given us the musical equivalent of special effects movies in the form of "heavy metal" rock concerts—in which bands produce shoddy but extremely loud music—so loud that it is damaging to the ears, so loud that it can be felt as well as heard. It disengages genuine attention. There is no need to *listen* to the music. Gaudy makeup and overblown special effects serve to distract the audience from the music's lack of subtlety and substance. To complete the mental escape, attendees often ingest mind-numbing drugs.

The musical equivalent of "reality" shows comes in the form of offensive lyrics, largely emanating from practitioners of such styles as "gangsta rap." Their behavior is regarded as an exercise in freedom of expression because it is a predominately black idiom (thus representative of American cultural diversity). Ostensibly, such music is a natural and justified response to generations of white male oppression. In truth, most rap is simply juvenile, abusive, and desensitizing. It emphasizes sex, violence, and "shock value" and seldom offers a meaningful message. But in a postmodern world, who's to say?

Postmodernism has undermined the concept of elders.

Civilization is, in many respects, an artificial construct. Its preservation depends upon our ability to indoctrinate the youth. But, if all opinions are equal, then children's opinions are just as valid as those of adults. This misconception—born during the 60's when college students thought they knew more than their teachers—has led schools to evaluate teachers based upon student surveys. When students evaluate teachers, popularity becomes crucial, reducing the teacher's status to something on the order of prom queen candidate. And who's a popular teacher? Someone who "identifies" with the students, who is a buddy rather than a mentor, who is lenient in grading and attendance policies, who willingly dilutes a syllabus in order to attract students—in short, someone who expects less to educate than to "relate"—is, by postmodern standards, a better teacher, *regardless of academic results.* Initially, student activists coerced institutions to adopt this policy—sometimes violently. Since then, the new notion of students' rights has been maintained by the schools themselves, in part as a result of pressure to increase tuition revenues and in part because the students of the 60's are now school administrators.

In fact, age discrimination is intended to work *for* the young, not *against* them. Its aim is to protect them, not to punish them. It helps us to provide them with what we *know* they need rather than what they *believe* they need. There are reasons that we send kids to school, that we restrict their behavior via age limits for driving, smoking, alcohol consumption, and so on. We, as adults, understand that they have much to learn and they're not yet ready to enter the adult world. While it is true that maturation rates vary among individuals, data such as insurance company actuarial tables clearly indicate that age discrimination serves a meaningful purpose. On the whole, children and adolescents are demonstrably less rational than adults. Their opinions are uninformed by experience and distorted by hormonal imbalances. Their success as adults depends in large part on their ability to assimilate some basic skills and facts while they're in school. Their first responsibility is to learn from functional adults how to become functional adults.

In the postmodern world, the percentage of students who graduate is a major factor in determining the quality of a school system, but children are no longer as accountable for learning. This leads to the unwarranted promotion and eventual graduation of unskilled and illiterate youth. Having abandoned corporal punishment and curtailed most other forms of negative reinforcement, the public school system now seeks to appease students. It wants nothing more than to keep them safe, calm, and quiet. Learning has become a lesser priority. Much of the appeasement involves "edutainment" and "relating." The postmodern educator's emphasis on social interaction and teamwork is remarkably convenient. In a postmodern school, where values are more important than facts, answers are less likely to be judged right or wrong. Different answers simply represent different perspectives. This conveniently reduces the teacher's need for subject matter expertise.

The first generation of postmodernism's failed experiment is now teaching the second. Cheating, which has been rampant for two decades, has become institutionalized because many of the new teachers were practitioners of the art and don't see the harm in it. Recent major scandals reveal that many public schools and even entire municipal school systems are now cheating *for* their students in order to bring up system-wide test averages. And why not, after all? Who's to say?

Shortsighted postmodern solutions cause new problems.

If blacks generally do not perform as well on standardized tests as whites, then the standardized tests must be racially biased. So they must be "revised" (codeword for "diluted"). And, if blacks graduate from high school, then they must be ready for college and should, therefore, be represented in commensurate numbers (hence quotas). If college admission standards are too high, then they must be "revised" as well. The SAT was initially diluted during the late 70's to make it less "culturally biased" (meaning "too hard"). That alone was insufficient. The typical American university now allows something on the order of a 100 to 200 point SAT handicap for blacks. Some schools also apply *negative* handicaps for Asians, because Asians generally perform *too well* relative to whites, especially in technical fields.

Results: Based on race, incompetent students are often admitted and competent students are often turned away. Our universities are burdened with the task of teaching high school level material during the first two years of baccalaureate programs. They dilute coursework in order to graduate the unqualified students they've admitted. To do otherwise might *appear* discriminatory and could be financially ruinous thanks to the litigious enforcement of political correctness. But mere dilution of coursework is insufficient, so schools often ignore cheating and, thereby, permit incompetent students to pass.

Old institutional injustices (e.g., racial segregation) have been replaced by new ones (e.g., handicapping schemes). The new ones are demeaning to those women and minority members who are able to compete success-fully on a level playing field—people who bear the undeserved stigma of tokenism (e.g., "great woman composer" instead of simply "great com-poser"). Useful and just solutions to social inequities include extracurricu-lar tutoring, special mentoring programs, tuition assistance, and so forth—opportunities for disadvantaged kids to "pull up some slack" and succeed where their parents failed. But these things alone aren't quick or easy enough for postmodernists.

Postmodern revisionist history is divisive and dishonest.

White men were, in fact, responsible for most of the major advances in science, the arts, industry, and technology that have occurred during the past few hundred years. They also lead the fight to abolish rigid class struc-tures, thereby paving the way for others to share in a more humane world. It's important to realize that the people of the past were constrained by their social contexts. In much of the world the old inequities persist, despite the presence of a more humane Western model. Our ancestors had no such model. They were essentially powerless to overrule the dictates of monarchs and church leaders anyway. I'm not trying to justify the past. The overt and institutional bigotry that persisted into the 60's in the South, for example, was inexcusable. Some white men were, indeed, big-ots. Some still are. But stereotyping white males is no more appropriate than stereotyping blacks or women.

It's more productive to concern ourselves with the present than to rewrite the past for political efficacy. It's easy to criticize the behavior of our ancestors, but they lived in a world that was radically different from ours. That women and minorities now have greater opportunities to par-ticipate is what's really important. It's time to make peace and forge ahead. There are many blacks and women who *can* compete on a level playing field. The current mindset isn't progressive. It's just patronizing.

THE POSTMODERN MUSICAL LANDSCAPE

Long ago, American popular music adopted many of the principles developed by literary composers of the Classical Era. For example, Scott Joplin's rags quite clearly employ Classical voice leading principles and common practice functional harmony—albeit with a distinctly different flavor. As jazz matured and combos grew into stage bands, arrangers also incorporated some of the more recent features of literary music such as extended tertian chords and clear grouping of instruments by families. During the big band era, arrangers developed considerable skill in scoring. That skill persists because the concept of elders applies in jazz.

The most significant weakness of jazz is its lack of development. In jazz, as in the folk music from which it arose, emphasis remains on homophonic exposition of basic material, although jazz sometimes offers extended dramatic shape by way of improvisation. Improvisation, however, is less precise than composition and, consequently, is prone to lapses of judgment. For that reason, improvisation is often carefully worked out in advance so that it appears spontaneous but, in fact, isn't.

Some of the more sophisticated jazz styles have adopted some aspects of modernism (e.g., be-bop) but most have successfully avoided the more extreme techniques. I think this avoidance can be attributed to the improvisatory skills of jazz musicians, whose ears simply wouldn't allow them to go "whole hog" because they instinctively strove for audible order. Even so, they were accused of being "too cerebral"—for exactly the same reason that the phrase was applied (albeit incorrectly) to the modernists in academia. All in all, then, the shortcomings of jazz are fairly minor and, in fact, most jazz is significantly more musical than a great deal of academic modernist music.

A serious problem arose with the advent of rock and roll. Players suddenly became much younger. They borrowed the barest skeleton of harmony from other styles—relying almost exclusively on root position I, IV, and V chords. Most had only the barest instinctive grasp of internal voice leading—a shortcoming that generally persists.

Most rockers lack the knowledge that harmony is a byproduct of the subtle interactions between distinct lines with independent melodic contours. In terms of the progress paradigm, rock harmonization is at best a setback to pre-Classical times. Because rock "elders" are mostly untrained kids from the previous decade, such problems persist. There's far less counterpoint and development in rock than in jazz—largely because most rock is constructed via improvisation without recourse to notation. On the whole, the fairly modest drawbacks of jazz are amplified (literally and figuratively) in rock. Rock's nearly universal lack of skilled arrangers persists because so many of its young, musically illiterate players simply "jam" in their garages in hopes of crudely assembling "hits." Rock's musical shortcomings are exacerbated because "star" selection is based more on physical appearance and overt sexuality than on musical prowess.

The concept of elders facilitates an ongoing search for improvements. So styles naturally change over time because of insights and innovations. But the music industry's motivation for changing styles is a marketing strategy. It's based on the commercial concept of planned obsolescence. The basic formula is: "new decade = new style." A new style needn't be better. It just has to be *different*—so that it can be characterized as "rebellious" and marketed to the latest batch of adolescents as "their" music.

Postmodernism inclusiveness prohibits judgment.

The pervasive politically correct view regarding controversy favors *inclusiveness*. This seems quite innocuous and accommodating at the surface, especially in a society that values freedom of expression. It's overtly democratic. Offhand, it sounds downright equitable. The politically correct view is that differing opinions *must* be tacitly accepted as equally valid because all qualitative judgment regarding the arts is fraught with social, political, and ethnic biases. Hence, "It's art if I say it is."

Postmodern inclusiveness supports the "pops" mistake.

The "pops" phenomenon, with help from the current emphasis on political correctness, has blurred the distinction between popular and literary music and, if unchecked, will continue to erode public interest in and awareness of the latter. This problem has been exacerbated by a decline in the quality of popular music—which has increased the qualitative gap between popular music and literary music. Popular musicians have gradually become younger and less musically literate over the past several decades. This is a direct and intentional consequence of the music industry's marketing strategy—which is to target adolescents. As the qualitative gap between popular and literary music widens, serious literature (including the war-horses) becomes less comprehensible to general audiences and, therefore, less relevant. The politically correct climate has unwittingly served the music industry very well by way of a self-contradictory but subtle argument: All opinions are equal; therefore, the only measure of validity is in the number of people who share an opinion (i.e., the only justifiable measure of quality is popularity—which is directly measured in sales). And since the industry decides what to market, it also decides what will be popular.

The argument emphasizing popularity is particularly seductive in a society that measures value in dollars and cents. The music industry routinely grants awards based on popularity and people pay extraordinary ticket fees to attend concerts involving popular "artists." Worse still, symphony orchestras validate this view by performing popular music and by presenting popular entertainers as guest "artists." Opera companies validate it by presenting Broadway musicals alongside works by Puccini and

Wagner. *Why, after all, would such bastions of high culture perform the music of Andrew Lloyd Webber if it were schlock?*

Trained musicians have "gut" feelings regarding what works and what doesn't in a piece of music. We have favorite pieces and favorite passages, but we have difficulty verbalizing why. Or we believe that it would take too long to explain, or that, by explaining we would appear confrontational or snobby or condescending, so we avoid the topic. This leads to a tendency among trained musicians to apologize for their expertise and to concede that their attraction to "stuffed shirt" music is simply an acquired taste. In this way, without necessarily subscribing to the inclusive view, serious musicians can contribute to its strength. Ultimately, by apologizing for expertise and avoiding the "snob" label, they validate the "reverse snobbery" position, which claims qualitative superiority based on popularity. When serious ensembles perform popular literature (in "pops" concerts), the performers themselves participate in that validation. This occurs largely via financial coercion. Because literary music is unpopular, seriously trained musicians are, on the whole, poorly compensated. And serious ensembles need to sell tickets in order to stay in business. The prevailing attitude seems to be that they can only attract audiences by offering inferior but familiar literature *and anything is better than nothing.*

Postmodern inclusiveness supports reverse snobbery.

The inclusive position has fostered its own brand of *exclusivity* as well, in the form of *reverse snobbery.* If someone expresses a preference for serious literature, the reverse snob can hastily label the offender a "snob," an "elitist," or a "Euro-centrist," and thus preempt any threat of actual mental engagement. It's a convenient way to avoid confronting one's own ignorance and it's perfectly acceptable in the age of sound bites. In fact, the person invoking the "snob" pejorative is automatically granted the moral high ground.

Interestingly, one is not likely to be called a snob for preferring a particular popular style (e.g., country-western, hip-hop, reggae, industrial). So it's fairly clear that the "snob" label is actually a defensive tool that arises from the denial of one's own intellectual shortcomings. A snob, you see, is someone who prefers music that requires some formal knowledge to fully comprehend. You can prefer *anything else* and simply be regarded as an individual with specific tastes. You can even like classical music without being a snob, *but only if you like something else just as much.*

> There is in the contemporary American character a disturbing tendency to take the easiest possible path in life…Should the artist only meet us on our own emotional and intellectual level? If that were the case, we would have been denied the *Goldberg Variations,* the *Rite of Spring, Don Giovanni,* Verdi's *Requiem*—the list goes on. This disdain for struggle is responsible in no small way for the interest in minimalism and New Age music. These egocentric extensions of the drug culture find their allure in escape, not aspiration. Perhaps this is one of the conditions which caused British film producer David Putnam to offer this sobering view of contemporary America: "There is a disillusionment wafting through the heady winds of the American dream as more and more people come to feel that they've had the experience but somehow, somewhere, missed out on the meaning of it."[30]

The politically correct brand of inclusiveness is actually *exclusive.* It opposes contrary opinions and it especially opposes serious concert literature on the grounds that it is elitist, Euro-centric, and symptomatic of white male oppression. In practice inclusiveness has provided PBS and NPR with an excuse to improve their ratings by programming popular music for "balanced coverage". Commercial radio stations have conspicuously failed to reciprocate by programming art music, so the net effect has been that public broadcasting has simply come to resemble commercial broadcasting. Commerce has won out over artistry and, given time, such "inclusiveness" will probably result in death to public broadcasting. Why, after all, should the public support a system that duplicates the programming of self-sustaining commercial stations?

Although they sound noble and democratic, the terms "inclusiveness" and "balanced coverage" are examples of postmodern American Newspeak. They justify the inclusion of that which is most popular (hence most financially viable) and the exclusion of that which is not. They're good for political efficacy and for profits, but they are of no value for the arts.

Postmodernism has politicized arts funding.

Although literary music is generally better crafted, more elegantly proportioned, more intellectually stimulating, more effective at representing the natural hierarchy of biological rhythm, it is not very important in the average citizen's daily life. It's unpopular. Therefore, its practitioners are called elitists.

Postmodern cultural relativism has required that the artistic merits of European literary music be downplayed and that other, more widely enjoyed styles be elevated to higher status. In other words, that which is popular must be perceived as *elite*. It would be insufficient merely to point out (correctly) that literary music isn't very popular. That wouldn't weaken its significance *as art*. It is necessary to negate its historical significance *as art* in order to elevate the historical significance of popular music *as art*. Why? Because white European males wrote the literary war-horses. The new "inclusive" position holds that folk and popular music, especially that produced by women, minorities, and non-westerners, has been misunderstood, under-appreciated, and under-represented because of white male oppression. It requires a claim that the historical "deification" of white male composers who wrote most of the recognized literary masterpieces was sexist and racist. In short, it requires replacing an objective truth (that the war horses are great works) with politically motivated lies (that quality is simply a matter of opinion and the literary war-horses are sexist and racist).

The original mission of the National Endowment for the Arts was to protect and preserve that art which, although unpopular, *deserved* protection. But in the new social agenda, literary music no longer deserved protection, so the NEA looked for something else to protect and preserve (in order to protect and preserve its own staff and budget). In the rush to be politically correct—to avoid budget cuts and possible outright elimination—the NEA shifted its funding emphasis from high art to projects befitting the new social agenda. Postmodernism jeopardized the NEA's future by making high art unworthy of protection and then rescued it by redefining what *was* worthy: If the value of art is not intrinsic to the art itself, then the value of art must be in its ability to serve social causes—that is, the value of art must be *political.* Postmodern art is better, therefore, if it addresses issues associated with women and minorities, gays and lesbians, cultural diversity, environmental issues, and so forth—*regardless of craft.*

The NEA wasn't alone in adopting this strategy. NPR and PBS capitulated as well. And, of course, state and local arts agencies followed suit because they receive strings-attached money from the NEA. They, in turn, distribute money to individual artists and arts organizations whose grant proposals fit the new social mission. He who has the gold makes the rule.

The new agenda doesn't end there. In order to facilitate it, the playing field must be unleveled. When organizations compete for funds, there must be an advantage to members of the oppressed and, therefore, deserving groups (i.e., anybody except white heterosexual males). So a proposal to commission a black lesbian to write an opera that depicts a slave woman's struggle to escape the antebellum South via the Underground Railroad is much more likely to be funded than a proposal to commission a white man to write a symphony—*regardless of the relative abilities of the composers in question.* Why? Because the postmodern qualitative measure of art is political.

The current institutionalized patronization suggests that women and blacks *can't* compete on a level playing field—an insinuation that surely insults those who *can.* The odds of success as a composer, regardless of color or gender, are easily 1000 to 1 against. So, why should any particular group be given an advantage? Nazi and Soviet governments intruded in the realm of music composition for political reasons, as do the many oppressive societies that still exist. Postmodernists understand that such intrusions elsewhere are wrong, but apparently they can't understand that politicizing the arts here and now is wrong as well.

Most "world music" is simply imitation American rock.

If you tune into NPR programs these days, you're likely to hear some "alternative" or "world music". The postmodern misconception of "multiculturalism" led directly to this programming policy. At one time, NPR music selection acknowledged that literary music, while not popular enough to be financially viable, was of great cultural value and, therefore, deserved to be preserved. Now, however, literary music—especially that written by white European males—has been categorized as racist and sexist and, consequently, undeserving. So postmodernists have implemented a policy of *inclusiveness*. Now any style of music that is not heavily represented by U.S. commercial record companies is "alternative" music and, therefore, deserves preservation.

Throughout the 20th Century, ethnomusicologists recorded extensive collections of folk music from around the world. The records are stored in University music libraries and seldom accessed, except by musicology majors. Most true world music really isn't particularly appealing to Western ears. Because non-Western scales are structured differently from ours, they often sound out of tune to us. The recordings are field recordings, not studio recordings, so they haven't been "sweetened" by technicians. The instruments are typically odd, primitive, and acoustically inferior. The languages are foreign. The rhythms are unfamiliar and harmony is generally omitted altogether. Needless to say, true world music doesn't have much of a market here. Nonetheless, multiculturalism dictates that world music should be performed.

This posed a conundrum until the music industry came to the rescue: If NPR listeners don't want *real* world music, why not give 'em *fake* world music—something that pleases the untrained Western ear, something that lets American populists "relate" to their foreign brothers, something that makes 'em feel artsy and sophisticated without a lot of actual effort. How, you ask? Go to developing countries and offer recording contracts to popular bands that play good old rock 'n' roll with just a bit of local color for seasoning. Find bands that use American electric guitars, keyboards, amplifiers, and drum sets, but also use some folk instruments for "seasoning." Find bands that use characteristic rock melodic and harmonic structure, but maybe with a slightly different "feel." If you can find 'em, use bands that sing in English but with heavy, colorful accents.

In other words, give back to Americans a slightly imperfect mirror of our own popular music. That is surely the way to win our hearts. Now, rock, hip-hop, rap, and various other popular styles of music can regularly be heard on NPR stations. It's world music, after all, so it deserves to be programmed. And—conveniently—it's great for ratings. But literary music is losing airtime. And true world music is gradually being replaced by a homogenized, Americanized, processed music substitute.

Above all, postmodern Americans want multiculturalism to be easy and convenient. The new NPR strategy saves people from the effort of actually engaging their minds when attempting to understand other cultures around the globe. This simplistic postmodern variety of "world music" reveals that multiculturalism isn't really what it purports to be. Its real aim is homogeneity—global "McDonaldization" rather than true recognition and acceptance of foreign cultures. It provides a handy new source of products to peddle here and helps to open up a broader foreign market for American products. The main thing is that it helps the music industry's bottom line. Because imitation American rock around the world represents multiculturalism, real American rock here at home does as well. If properly packaged, trite adolescent music can be passed off as significant art:

National Public Radio…can hardly go a week without featuring some young, articulate commentator as "rock critic" who'll regale listeners with their observations on the profound significance of the latest release by whatever band is their current discovery. They'll ascribe social and aesthetic virtues to awful music that should serve as cautionary examples of what results when musical instruments are given to adolescents without supervision.[31]

Commentators have also contributed to the problem.

To the general public, critics are authority figures. Yet some critics are only slightly more musically astute than their readers. The justification for this is the ridiculous notion of critic-as-everyman. The basic proposition is, "If I, the critic, am just like everybody else and I like this piece, then many others will like it, too. Therefore, my opinion is a valid reflection of the quality of the piece as the public will likely perceive it." This is convenient and attractive for unschooled music critics because it provides justification for asserting personal preferences without the need for genuine expertise.

Gimmicks often sway critics. If a composer with dubious craft brainstorms and comes up with a new technique (putting the performers in the hall and the audience on stage, say), some lame-brained critic will marvel at the cleverness of the "innovation" and rave about it in his review—especially if he can extract a load of pseudo-philosophical patter from the program notes ("Who's to say where the music *really* comes from, after all?").

In the postmodern world, there's no need to be right if you can't be proven wrong. This plays very nicely into the music industry's hand. If a critic-as-everyman gives a new piece a good review, then the music industry can turn on its hype machine and convert the composer into a "star." The lucky composer's music is suddenly in demand everywhere. And, in response to financial pressures, major ensembles everywhere program it, so it is validated without regard to its intrinsic merit. With no objective standards for evaluating music, the *de facto* standard becomes popularity (i.e., record sales).

Critics have power. They exert a great deal of influence on public opinion. They can essentially "make or break" composers. And, too often, with power comes arrogance. Consider this remark by *The New York Times* chief music critic, Bernard Holland:

> [Kyle] Gann is understandably fearful of European cultural oppression and the inferiority complexes it has caused. His fears are justified by the vast mediocrity most American concert composers continue to offer. It is a mediocrity supported not by Americans in general but by philanthropic cultural minority, and that without much enthusiasm.[32]

This statement is exceedingly presumptuous. Holland, like the general public, is clearly unaware of the vast wealth of American concert music. Holland's position represents both ignorance and prejudice. Not only have there been many American composers whose brilliance is broadly acknowledged (e.g., Barber, Ives, Bernstein, Copland, and *many* more), but also there are several thousand living Americans whose music is rarely performed and who, consequently, have no avenue for gaining recognition.

Like critics in general, Holland has no idea who we are, let alone what we've written, but he presumes to know that it's mediocre. Actually, he only hears concert music by composers who've been anointed more or less randomly by mediocre *critics* because composers who lack critical acclaim also lack opportunities for exposure. One of the great misfortunes of music journalism is that there are no standard prerequisites for the job of critic. If Holland were himself a composer, he would certainly be better informed regarding the quality of our work. Unfortunately, because he writes for *The New York Times*, reviewers elsewhere are likely to regard his opinions as important and authoritative. Holland's remarks also reflect a *real* cultural bias:

> Gann and his cohorts are getting it from both directions. As long as they write for symphony orchestras, opera houses and traditional concert settings, they remain colonists. The instruments and formats these institutions use are products of other people's thoughts and tendencies, summations of their histories: namely, European histories.[32]

From Holland's perspective, it is apparently impossible to write good, original American concert literature because even to attempt it is to be a "colonist." But American folk music—including the Negro spirituals that significantly influenced early jazz—is also very strongly rooted in the European tradition and has virtually no connection elsewhere. It employs European tertian harmony, European period-structure melodies and, where instruments apply, European instruments. In fact, European common practice is more clearly reflected in American folk and popular music than it is in modern American concert music. Furthermore, many Americans have links to Europe in the "summations of our histories." This is a simple historical fact, not a culturally biased opinion. However competent Holland may be as a critic of European common practice performance, his judgment is clouded by a prejudice against American concert literature, so he should avoid reviewing new American works.

The following excerpt from an article by Sheldon Atovsky demonstrates some of the consequences of succumbing to postmodernism on the matter of criticism:

> Industrial music is also pervasively neglected by scholars. The neglect is due to many reasons…There is a bias in the intellectual community toward this style of music and toward most other styles of music that are not embraced by the high music culture industry. Teachers and scholars of music most often do not keep up with changes in musical language which occur after they finish their studies and consequently do not critically listen to it…Finally, paraphrasing the critic Robert Christgau in *The Village Voice* (1991): music criticism, which would be a useful tool to approach this music, is held in low regard by music scholars in favor of a more scientific/analytical approach and thus they do not know where to begin to find an approach to understanding this music.[33]

According to Atovsky, academics can't understand popular music—which is like saying that literary novelists can't understand comic books. Atovsky also asserts that criticism would be more useful than analysis. So, he implies that opinion is more useful than fact. In truth, there is nothing about popular music that precludes the use of academic analytical techniques.

Academic theorists have a broad array of tools available for analyzing music; their efficacy is not confined to the study of common-practice music. Furthermore, analysis yields objective, measurable, verifiable information, whereas criticism is quite subjective. Although the critic's conclusion ("This is a great piece"—meaning "I liked it" or "This is a terrible piece"—meaning "I didn't like it") may turn out to be correct, the primary tool at his disposal is opinion, which, because it is subjective, settles nothing. Could it be that a music theorist's more "scientific/analytical approach" might yield a more precise understanding and evaluation than the critic's subjective approach? Yes, of course. But the postmodernist prefers to leave evaluation in the realm of subjectivity rather than undertake an arduous but objective inquiry.

Radio commentary and program notes are often geared toward extramusical anecdotes surrounding the creation of a particular piece—recent deaths in the composer's family, diseases he suffered from, his mood, his sex life, his financial state, and so forth. One might get the impression that the composer's breakfast menu was more important than his method of choosing the notes. This just isn't true. If mood swings influence our writing so much, how do we manage to sustain specific moods for the weeks, months, or even years we spend writing some pieces? Why do we recognize a composer's style regardless of where he lived while writing a particular piece and regardless of the attendant events in his personal life? The salient information about a piece of music is in its content, not in the composer's personal life. Extramusical information tends, if anything, to obfuscate the meaning of the music itself. Biographical information gives the audience nothing to listen for, no road map for the experience, no tools for comprehension. If critics and disk jockeys were better equipped to understand the music themselves, they'd be more capable of guiding audiences toward rewarding concert experiences.

THE POSTMODERN MISTAKE

Postmodernism exalts trite music rooted in popular idioms and postmodern political pressure has dragged inferior works into our concert halls. Unfortunately, the music industry has successfully imposed its "pop" marketing strategy into the world of concert music. In particular, three categories of shallow music have been elevated to the status of "high art" as a result of postmodern tactics: minimalism, New Age music, and crossover music. Imitation "world music" is not far behind. New Age and minimalist music can both be traced back to the 60's search for Eastern and alternative mysticism and for drug-induced escape from reality. Crossover music is just popular music "dressed up" by changing the instrumentation. All three categories offer mood without substance. Ironically, while the West has been searching for answers in the East, Asians have come to recognize and embrace the mainstream literary tradition. Their children now study violin, piano, and composition with a seriousness of purpose that is largely missing here.

Hyperbole has distorted the concept of concert music.

In this country, where the free market is cherished, we have come to equate value with commercial viability. But this is a flawed equation. There is usually a lag of years or even decades between the advent of a really important new musical style and its acceptance by the public. Many people—especially older people like our graying concert audiences—resist unfamiliar and challenging ideas. They prefer the comfortable, familiar ways, the old music. Yet the advancement of civilization depends upon the creative effort of those who challenge traditions. Nearly every advance that civilization makes is met with

155

resistance from the conservative masses. This is as true in literary music as it is elsewhere. Consider Nicolas Slonimsky's observation that a piece of music that is harshly criticized (particularly when the word "cacophonous" is used) is more likely to become an acknowledged masterpiece than a work that is moderately well received. This is not conjecture. It is history. Slonimsky also provided the following timetable for the acceptance of new music, based on his study of hundreds of 19th and early 20th Century reviews:

> A fairly accurate timetable could be drawn for the assimilation of unfamiliar music by the public and the critics. It takes approximately twenty years to make an artistic curiosity out of a modernistic monstrosity; and another twenty to elevate it to a masterpiece. Not every musical monstrosity is a potential musical masterpiece, but its chances of becoming one are measurably better than those of a respectable composition of mediocre quality.[34]

Actually, it is not true that a long period of time is required before a masterpiece can be recognized. Haydn didn't need forty years to recognize the young Mozart's genius. Schumann didn't accuse Brahms of writing monstrosities. Haydn and Schumann immediately understood the work of their younger colleagues because they, as elder composers, had thoroughly assimilated the progress paradigm. Slonimsky demonstrates that bad criticism is not new, but the postmodern "everyman" notion exacerbates the problem. Bad critics of the present, blissfully unaware of the effect their own bad judgment has, probably read Slonimsky's *Lexicon of Musical Invective* and chuckle over the idiotic pronouncements made by their incompetent predecessors.

The music industry hypocritically claims that it just gives the public what the public wants. In fact, the industry determines what the public wants because it has the financial clout to decide what the public hears. The public quite simply cannot want music that it has never heard. The industry prefers naïve consumers because they're easier targets. So the central thrust of its strategy is to choose new groups that can be "packaged" effectively and launch massive advertising campaigns that, through sheer size, essentially "black out" alternatives.

This strategy is supported by the news media, which are now largely owned by the entertainment industry and which depend upon advertising revenue for survival. And advertising revenue, in turn, depends upon ratings. This, in conjunction with the musical illiteracy of many critics, accounts for such things as "rave" newspaper reviews for rock concerts and unbridled hyperbole that is routinely presented as news. For example, on February 19, 2000, CNN Headline News aired an interview about the auction of John Lennon's piano in which the interviewee dubbed Lennon "the composer of the millennium." That moniker would rank him above every other composer since the late Medieval Era—a ludicrous proposition. The story was presented as news although it was clearly just a "plug" for the pending auction. Unfortunately, the public seems to lack sufficient skepticism regarding industry hyperbole.

> But undeniably, people do tend to react to purveyors as arbiters of what is good. Rightly or wrongly, in a Capitalist culture, the media giants are seen by many as the standard bearers of aesthetic values.[35]

The "crossover" phenomenon has further confused the public's understanding of the distinction between literary music and popular music. Since many people, including many classical radio station disk jockeys, apparently think that the distinction is merely a matter of instrumentation, orchestral and chamber arrangements of popular tunes receive frequent radio airplay on classical stations (e.g., imitation-Baroque string quartet arrangements of Beatles tunes). Programming works like Paul McCartney's *Liverpool Oratorio* helps to propagate this misconception of what modern literary music is. Actually, the self-professed musical illiterate McCartney made up tunes for the oratorio, but a fellow Brit named Carl Davis scored it. Since its 1991 premier by the Royal Liverpool Philharmonic, the work has been performed over 100 times in over 20 countries. This level of exposure is simply unavailable to even the most gifted of living literary composers. And every performance of a spurious work like this robs programming time from more serious endeavors—but it's good for the orchestra's "bottom line."

McCartney has fame and fortune, but now he also wants to be taken seriously as an artist, even though he obviously hasn't taken the composition process seriously himself. He's had the better part of a lifetime to learn rudimentary music theory but he hasn't even learned to *read* music. He could spend some of his money getting a musical education; to avoid public embarrassment, he could even hire live-in tutors. That, however, would require a private admission that he doesn't know what he's doing.

I've often heard it said that popular composers are just as serious as concert composers. It may be true that they work hard at the process of writing, but I find the argument unconvincing on quite another level: Concert composers have studied the great masters, learned to imitate their craft, and assimilated the great lessons of the past. Popular composers, although most of them are at least vaguely aware that great literature exists, do not avail themselves of its lessons. The process of acquiring a solid education in composition is a bit too arduous. It's much better to rely upon the hyperbole of the press for consolation than it is to recognize one's weaknesses and overcome them.

When a symphony orchestra invites a "pop" star to appear as a guest artist on a concert, that orchestra essentially validates the associated "literature" as especially worthy and the soloist as an important musician of our time. Simultaneously, it denigrates the reputations of its own players, who are far more qualified, by placing them in the role of "back up" accompanists. The decision to perform pops concerts is financially rather than artistically motivated, but the audience doesn't perceive it as such. The audience is gleefully unaware that it has been deprived of an opportunity to learn the real value of art, which is in the struggle to learn and grow—in short, to be uplifted rather than pampered and mollycoddled.

Ironically, one of the industry's hyperbole tactics is to label popular performers as "classically trained." This term is applied for anything from a few piano lessons during childhood to a year or two as an undergraduate music major, whereas a typical classical musician holds a master's or higher degree in performance and years or even decades of additional study with internationally recognized *virtuosi*. And a typical literary composer has a Ph.D. in composition and years of study with one or more major composers from the preceding generation. If classical training makes for better musicians, then thoroughly trained classical musicians should generally be better than popular musicians with just a smattering of musical training in their backgrounds. And, in fact, they are. But this is a conclusion that the public fails to reach because the public is largely unaware of the training that serious musicians undergo. Other words favored by the industry include "artist" and "innovator." The word "artist" is a pretentious substitute for "entertainer," and popular entertainers produce almost nothing truly innovative.

Fads with catchy labels like "minimalism," "New Age," and "crossover" are easily marketed to unsuspecting consumers. Such gimmicks readily dupe journalists, including many critics, as well. And once an incompetent composer has established himself via a "rave" review, the concert world becomes his oyster. Thanks to an "Emperor's New Clothes" mindset, one good review begets another: If an influential reviewer wrongly praises a musical charlatan, subsequent reviewers generally follow suit to conceal their own ignorance. So more rave reviews lead to repeat performances and increased record sales. And since members of the music industry administer the high-profile music awards, the awards are based primarily on record sales.

The industry invites the media to cover their awards presentations (which are actually publicity events for the industry itself) and the media dutifully announce the names of award recipients *(as news)* to the public. So the public spends more money buying more CDs—increasing the momentum of a self-perpetuating cycle of more performances followed by more awards followed by more publicity. The music industry throws in some carefully scripted interviews and a few appearances on TV talk shows in which the "artist" ladles out some impressive-sounding pseudo-intellectual patter and soon he's dubbed "important." In short order, the "important artist" becomes a "star," then a "superstar," and then an "icon." And, of foremost importance, the music industry enhances its bottom line.

The industry might just as easily tap any one of thousands (or tens of thousands) of contenders for the "star" role; the exact choice isn't all that important. The marketing strategy and the packaging (including a pretentious pseudo-intellectual label) are actually more important than the product itself. So "getting the big break" has more in common with winning a lottery than with proving one's artistic merit.

Once the "star" billing is filled (temporarily), it's not necessary to look elsewhere. There's no need to review thousands of unpublished recordings and unperformed scores in order to locate the best existing new American music. This is very fortunate for the music industry folks, because they wouldn't recognize it anyway. One insidious consequence of this is that the public—including many critics—now perceives American literary music as mediocre. They only hear a tiny sample of it because the industry only launches a few stars at a time (better for the marketing "blitz"). It isn't a particularly good sample, either; it's just what the industry has deemed most marketable based on its very limited research and equally limited musical taste.

Minimalist concert music exhibits remarkably poor craft.

In my earlier chapters on the psychology of music and on the progress paradigm of music history, I related many of the specific advances that have been made during the past millennium. The basic principle at work is that the composers in each successive generation have learned from their predecessors and contributed to an ongoing discourse, gradually and painstakingly improving our ability to create effective works. Now I'd like to show how an icon of the postmodern concert music world measures up to the task.

Philip Glass is possibly the best known of all the minimalists. Although he wasn't the first, he was probably the first to cultivate a public aura of mystique. He received a bachelor's degree in philosophy and mathematics (a "must" for the serious composer) from the University of Chicago. Then he spent four years at Juilliard. I don't know what he studied there or, for that matter, whether he actually studied at all, but I do know that he learned very little. Like many concert composers, he went to France to study with Nadia Boulanger. Again, he learned very little. Unlike most concert composers, he then traveled to India to study with Ravi Shankar. This led to his "artistic breakthrough." The following is an excerpt from Glass's *Mad Rush*. This passage isn't a fluke, by the way. It's representative of the entire work and, for that matter, of his output in general:

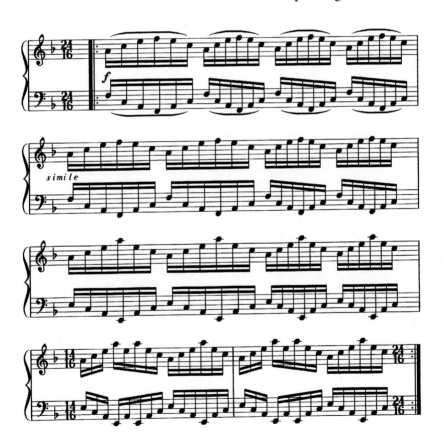

All eight beats of measures 1 and 2 are identical. They outline an F Major 7 chord via arpeggios in contrary motion. All four beats of measure 3 are identical. They continue to outline basically the same chord, but the highest note of the upper arpeggio is raised from F to A and the lowest note of the lower arpeggio is lowered from F to E, so that the root is omitted. In measures 4 and 5, The meter changes and the two outer notes of the respective arpeggios are repeated, which results in a very fleeting "hiccup" of slight rhythmic interest. The passage contains two lines of continuous slurred arpeggios in contrary motion outlining a single chord. It is constructed from constant note values and sustained at a constant dynamic level (forte). It is, consequently, extremely static. The entire passage is repeated—not to reinforce information. That's already been done. It's simply repeated to double its length.

This passage does fit music's definition because it portrays rhythm to some degree—although it's virtually devoid of hierarchy. By incessantly repeating a single basic figure with only trivial variations (Glass would prefer "subtle" rather than "trivial," I'm sure), it conveys its meaning to the listener. And its grammar is, of course, quite consistent. But it conveys almost no information at all. Measure 4 alone very nearly represents the entire message. The incessant repetition doesn't communicate the rhythm of human life so much as it suggests the drone of factory machinery.

Ostensibly, Glass's music is important literature that is informed by his study of ancient Eastern mysticism. Actually, this excerpt, which is representative of his output in general, is a monotonously repeated arpeggio based entirely on the notes of a decidedly European F Major 7 chord. This music may be purported to facilitate a meditative state or trance—something that could be served just as well by listening to your refrigerator hum. Its remarkable lack of character, direction, significant patterns, and dramatic shape might well engender a state of aural habituation—of hearing without listening. Like the rock music that gave it birth, minimalism is probably best taken with drugs because its purpose is escape rather than engagement. I'm reminded of Samuel Johnson's description of music as a way of "employing the mind without the labor of thinking at all." At best, this excerpt's appeal might lie at the shallow end of Copland's "sensuous plane." Although Mr. Glass has a large following, his writing exhibits extremely poor craft. Unfortunately, his marketability as a minimalist icon was sufficient to gain him an exclusive recording contract with CBS Masterworks—the first such contract since Aaron Copland's.

On the whole, minimalist music consists of undifferentiated homogeneity, which, as Leonard Meyer observed, gives rise to no relationships and consequently, no significant patterns. For an audience to participate vicariously in the composition process, the music must provide both unity and contrast. Because the patterns in minimalist music are insignificant, they are also disengaging. One could just as easily discover significant meaning in a sheet of sandpaper.

Popular music is unsuited for the concert hall.

Popular music serves a utilitarian function. It gives kids the opportunity to socialize. It's rooted in adolescent dance rituals. Because it's intended to accompany social dancing, the presence of a strong, steady beat is appropriate and the absence of meaningful development is understandable. Even so, the trend toward younger and younger performers is disturbing because it lowers the bar unnecessarily. And, via rock concerts and music videos, the industry has created the illusion that rock is significant listening material.

Before the 20th Century, the popular idiom was folk music. The elder fiddlers, pipers, and banjo pickers taught their children to play. Indeed, many folk musicians were quite accomplished. During the first half of the 20th Century, jazz was America's popular music. It was rooted in the same sort of oral tradition as folk music and it progressed owing to the adoption of music notation and to the age and maturity of its practitioners. However, the shift of popularity from jazz to rock and roll essentially unraveled the concept of elders as it applied to popular music. Now youngsters with no knowledge, no training, and no guidance from their elders are thrust into the spotlight. They don't need musical skills to impress their adolescent peers. Audacity is sufficient.

But "crossover" is primarily transplanted popular music.

The problem with crossover music is that it has dragged unschooled adolescent music into our concert halls. In his web-based article entitled "Don't Crossover Beethoven," Mark Ryan presents a fairly good account of its impact:

> Until recently the relative standing of classical and pop music could be summarised like this: classical stood on the summits with a small but dedicated following, while pop sloshed around with the hordes at the base. Classical was respected and supposedly elitist, pop was rebellious and plebian. The distinction no longer seems so clear cut. While many classical musicians now appear unsure of their place at the top and are ready to come down and do business with the masses, pop at the same time has its eye on the summit…
>
> It sometimes seems not so much that pop and classical are switching places on the mountain, but that the mountain itself is being flattened, leaving representatives of both genres to wander aimlessly in the crater. One of the biggest recent growth areas in record sales lies in what is known as crossover or 'popsical', described by Newsweek in rather apocalyptic terms as 'the only future classical has.' Crossover has dissolved the rigid division which once existed between classical and pop. With few exceptions the results are dismal—for the simple reason that popsical is not a development in music.
>
> Popsical is primarily a development in accountancy. Record companies, faced with stagnant or falling classical record sales, are desperate to catapult their artists into a higher earning orbit. What started some years ago as an attempt to sex up certain soloists with salacious publicity shots has ended up with the sexing up of the music itself. The violinist Vanessa Mae and cellist Ofra Harnoy, for example, are now

making straight pop albums.

Another reason for the growth of popsical lies in the psychological difficulties facing washed-up pop stars. At some point in the autumn of their years a craving for *gravitas* seems to get the better of many of them. Either, like Paul McCartney and Billy Joel, they actually try to write classical music, or, like Sting and Elton John, they appear on stage with the likes of Pavarotti, as if to convince themselves that they too are great singers...

However, the most important influence is the general spirit of relativism which pervades our times...Today...few people have either the stomach or the belief to affirm the superiority of anything, especially if that superiority is associated in some way with elitist tastes. So classical is undergoing a regrading. It is not better, it is just different; just as jazz is different to soul is different to funk etc, etc. In this featureless landscape of musical difference classical has no right to a privileged position; it must be made relevant, and above all it must immerse itself in the free-flow of difference. Popsical is the result.

In reality, only the most hardened relativists really believe that classical is no better than pop. More likely, people who have a vague desire to 'get into' a bit of classical, but don't know where to start, think that Michael Bolton's intense look or Vanessa Mae's pout will give them a leg up. Unfortunately it will probably have the opposite effect. The appeal of popsical indicates a hope that an appreciation of great music can be reached without too much effort or intellectual exertion. Relativism acts as little more than a cover for this type of laziness. The inner voice which stands ready to charge us with philistinism and willful stupidity can now be brushed off with the smug reassurance that there is no such thing as great music anyway.

Most of the classical repertoire is not readily appreciated and requires a struggle of the mind before it is assimilated into the senses. In these days of sound bites and reputedly short attention spans, the classical concert is an almost unique experience in the stillness and concentration it imposes on the listener for two or three hours…Superficial emotions place no demands on the intellect; in fact they are often antagonistic towards it. It is always the expression of the deepest human passions which engages and tests the intellect to the greatest extent…The danger in confusing the great currents of the deep with the froth on the surface is that we end up sweeping the whole lot together into one swirling torrent of garbage.[36]

New Age composers usually employ a great deal of repetition, although somewhat less than minimalists. Their music often drones away with steady 8th notes *ad nauseum* in mezzo-forte patterns akin to Alberti bass. Much of it is essentially bland accompaniment in the absence of significant patterns to accompany. The resultant texture is static, lacking in dramatic shape, and consequently prone to engendering habituation. The absence of rhythmic and melodic character in New Age melodic configurations is striking. Although the texture is monotonous, the listener may still experience difficulty trying to vicariously predict its course because the landscape is so featureless. It provides no compass—no significant patterns to recall, no melodic contour to predict.

Film scores, however effective as such, aren't concert works.

I should make it clear at the outset that when I refer to a film score, I mean music that was specifically fashioned as accompaniment to a film's action. A film score is entirely distinct from the juvenile "wall-to-wall" product placement of rock "hit tunes." The latter is a marketing ploy for selling both movies and albums. With very few exceptions (e.g., "rockumentaries" and "nostalgia trips"), such music intrudes upon the story, continually reminding the audience that it's just a movie. So its impact is to detract from the audience's ability to be absorbed into the story itself. In the most blatant abuses, vocal tunes are used at high volumes, so that the lyrics actually interfere with reception of the dialog.

Usually film scoring serves as rhythmic underpinning for a story. Film music can intensify the sense of foreboding in a suspenseful scene, the pastoral quality of a picnic, the passion of a love scene, the pace of a chase. By way of a steady beat, it can impart rhythmic continuity to a fairly disjunct succession of scenes. In a word, it can heighten the emotional impact of a movie and improve its flow. The similarities between music and drama that I already discussed should sufficiently explain why. Often a single instrument is used on a simple, repetitive melodic or rhythmic pattern—sometimes even just a single sustained pitch. It serves as "glue" to tie things together. At other times, just a brief bit of string tremolo can call attention to some important component of the story (e.g., the letter our protagonist walked right past on her way out of the apartment—the one she hasn't read yet—the one lying right there on the coffee table—the one from the killer).

Some film scores are quite striking and original. Much of the time, however, they're rather one-dimensional. Sometimes film scores are rip-offs of works by Stravinsky, Tchaikovsky, and others with superficial changes to the melodic material. It's important to realize that this usually happens not by the composer's choice but by the director's. While a film is being edited, it can be fitted with a "temp track" containing music from some other source (e.g., the director's personal CD collection). If the director likes the temp track, he may instruct the composer to write something that sounds almost identical. And sometimes film music composers imitate familiar non-Western and historical styles—quite appropriately—in order to fit the geographic and historical context of the story.

So, if film scores are generally effective, why don't they work in concerts? The answer is fairly simple: Film scoring is accompaniment. It borrows its dramatic shape from the film and it isn't intended to draw attention to itself. Even minimalist and New Age music, if used unobtrusively, can work in some film situations (e.g., when all that is required is a steady pulse to improve rhythmic coherence). On the whole, even title cues ("movie themes") are intended to establish mood and rhythmically unify the passing of the titles, not to acquire and hold the audience's attention. Many of Hollywood's orchestrators are highly skilled, to be sure. In fact, that's why composers like John Williams hire orchestrators like Herb Spencer to do their scoring. But the bottom line is this: If a film's music draws too much attention, then it intrudes into consciousness and detracts from the story. So, if it's written well, it doesn't engender attentive listening. There are exceptions, of course. At times the music is supposed to take the foreground (e.g., in portions of John Corigliano's score for *The Red Violin*—in which a violin is the main character).

Postmodern music has lowered the discourse.

A situation that somewhat resembled the postmodern reaction came at the end of the Baroque Era when the younger generation of composers reacted against what they perceived as too much complex counterpoint. Theirs was a shortsighted overreaction (albeit much more modest than the overreaction of the postmodernists). As the Classical Era matured, composers like Mozart reintroduced the contrapuntal complexity that the early classicists had rejected. Again, the historical lesson is fairly simple: The extent of a radical reaction is subsequently ameliorated. Over time, intensely reactionary works tend to become little more than historical curiosities. The reason for this is also fairly simple: Ever since the advent of notation, music has undergone a course of development that is self-monitoring and self-correcting. Despite the pendulum paradigm, progress has continued in more or less a straight line for scores of generations, so it has had ample opportunities to adjust. Its central path simply *cannot* be far off course. Therefore, a radical reaction against it is almost certainly wrong. Even minor reactions, although they tend to stimulate creativity, do not usually produce high art. The reactionary music of Bach's sons, for example, is fairly inconsequential when compared to the music that immediately preceded and followed it (High Baroque and mature Classical).

Postmodern music, however, is not simply a reaction within the world of concert music. It's an exercise in revisionist history—an attempt to deny that great music exists—because its very existence is an embarrassment to the current politically correct concept of equality. It's a pretentious little game of smoke and mirrors, nicely fashioned by the music industry to dupe the public. The industry's behavior isn't surprising; their motivation is to make money, after all. Quality is at best a secondary concern to them. Postmodernist composers would happily discard centuries of progress in exchange for Andy Warhol's fifteen minutes of fame—along with a few heaping wheelbarrow loads of cash. Hell, most of 'em don't really understand the great literature well enough to care what happens to it anyway. The real postmodern mistake is that they're being allowed to get away with it.

THE MAINSTREAM LITERARY ALTERNATIVE

The dogmas of the quiet past are inadequate to the stormy present.
The occasion is piled high with difficulty, and we must rise—with the occasion.

Abraham Lincoln: Annual Message to Congress, December 1, 1862.

Musical language evolves over extended periods, just as verbal language does. Attempts at extremely radical reform are fairly certain to fail because, like language, music is shared. The ability to convey musical meaning is limited not only by the composer's ability to conceive of a new musical language but also by the listener's ability to comprehend it. On the whole, the process of learning craft from our elders and then contributing to the ongoing discourse in incremental but meaningful ways has proven to be proper and productive. A modest reaction at the beginning of a new period stimulates creativity. It isn't particularly disruptive because the discrepancy between the periods is eventually ameliorated as the new period matures. As I showed earlier, this process naturally facilitates gradual but real progress. It insures that hard-gained knowledge is not lost and also allows its most creative practitioners to press ahead.

History's finest composers have contributed to music's progress. Hundreds of years ago monophony ruled—sometimes with the barest of rhythmic or harmonic accompaniment. Tunes were simple and rigidly structured. Orchestration was crude and primitive, as were the instruments themselves. Over time, literary music has become more complex, more fluid, more colorful, more exquisitely scored, and more expressive. Players and instruments, too, have improved—largely because of demands placed upon them by composers who have "pushed the envelope." In a word, music has progressed. It has done so because of the mainstream literary tradition, not because of the *avant-garde* and certainly not because of the postmodernists.

A grassroots movement is afoot that opposes both the pseudo-scientific approach of the modernists and the simple-minded gibberish of the postmodernists. Individual composers are writing in a variety of personal styles but with a common emphasis on musicality and craftsmanship. There is nothing new about this; most composers have continued to emphasize these traditional values throughout recent decades, despite the fact that our work has largely been ignored. Just as the intuitive mode quietly searches for patterns to present to our dominant verbal-analytical mode, mainstream composers have been quietly working while the dominant modern and postmodern movements have run their respective courses.

Mainstream literary music lacks gimmicks and labels.

However "catchy" fads and gimmicks may be, they've proven fruitless. Hopefully, the stage is now set for a re-emergence of public interest in musicality and craftsmanship—the hallmarks of mainstream literary music. Disappointed by both modernism and postmodernism but unaware of the alternative, some members of the general public have come to believe that either jazz or film music is "America's classical music." Composers have continued to work in the great tradition—albeit in relative solitude—throughout the 20th Century and onward to the present. During the past few decades, mainstream efforts have been eclipsed by the "glitzy" work of their *avant-garde* and postmodern contemporaries. And now, the inclusiveness doctrine, which is fundamentally an anti-intellectual backlash, threatens to undo centuries of progress by promoting trite pieces written by unschooled composers who have very little understanding of their historical legacy. Despite their lack of craft and substance, the minimalists *et al* have become the *de facto* successors to the *avant-garde*.

The present might well be called the "Age of the Consumer." Gimmicks and fads rule because they are easy to sell. Convenient labels are applied that serve as the musical equivalent of "sound bites." Inside academia, we've had *music concrete,* total serialism, stochastic music, aleatory music, et cetera. Outside, we now have minimalism, New Age, crossover, "world music," and various "alternative" labels. More recently we have post-minimalism, which lends further credence to minimalism. Why, after all would a movement be called "post-something" if the original "something" was unimportant? Moreover, post-minimalism gives the former practitioners of minimalism a new pedestal to stand on now that their old one has crumbled (because of shoddy construction).

Central to our study of historically significant cultures has been the examination of their art. The war-horse mindset is one that emphasizes the preservation of ancient masterpieces while failing to nurture its own art. This warped perspective denies the significance of the present and stifles our society's development at a time when creativity is sorely needed, not only in the arts, but in other facets of life as well. Our time, in turn, will be measured by its art—not by the art we've preserved from the common practice era. If our time is to contribute to the ongoing discourse, then the mainstream literary tradition must be revitalized and given the public attention that it deserves.

Mainstream literary composers have been shut out.

In an attempt to restore new mainstream literary music to its rightful place in our concert halls, disillusioned composers, both inside and outside of academia, have gradually become more vocal in challenging the intellectual supremacy of the *avant-garde.* However, progress is slow, because the *avant-garde* is so firmly entrenched. Furthermore, thanks to the music industry, the minimalists, New Age, and crossover composers have received some very high-profile public credit for spearheading the backlash against the *avant-garde.* Ostensibly, they're the rightful heirs to throne of "high art." As a consequence, mainstream literary composers—who were largely ignored while the *avant-garde* ruled—are now largely ignored because the minimalists rule.

Most composers are unknown, so our music is hard to find.

Based on various estimates, the number of living American composers is between about 8,000 and 32,000. My own personal estimate of *active* literary composers is much smaller—maybe 3,000, but it's still an enormous number relative to the few available performance opportunities. For my estimate, I presume that American composers are fairly evenly distributed, although there are significant concentrations in large metropolitan areas—especially in New York and Los Angeles. If my estimate is near the mark, there are roughly 60 active composers per state—with variations resulting largely from differences in state populations and concentrations of colleges and universities (since many serious composers also teach music theory and composition). Typical college music faculties include one or two composers while large university faculties often have three or four. The National Association of Composers, USA (NACUSA) has about 200 members. The Society of Composers, Inc. (SCI) and the American Composers' Forum have over 1,000 members each. But these rosters overlap (e.g., I am currently a member of both NACUSA and SCI). There are also many local and regional organizations, such as the Cleveland Composers Guild, the Tampa Bay Composers Forum, the Capital Composers Alliance, the Wisconsin Alliance for Composers (WAC), and the Southeastern Composers League.

These composer organizations publish newsletters that list recent performances of works by their members, so over time, I've accumulated a general impression of the kinds and numbers of activities in which members are involved. Most of the performance opportunities are in chamber music concerts on college campuses. Attendance at these events is made up largely of faculty, students, and fellow composers, and typically ranges from about 50 to 300 people. Although many concerts are recorded, most are not subsequently broadcast—not even locally. Because publicity is extremely limited and opportunities are few, most works receive very few performances (from zero to a dozen over several years) and are usually not published.

Mainstream literary composers share common experiences.

If you've read anything before by or about a composer, it was probably by or about one of the "stars" or one of the "well knowns." But they're rare. And many of them are, quite frankly, not very good composers. So, I think that a few observations from the peanut gallery might be useful—especially since most of us reside there.

Each composer's situation is, of course, unique in some respects, but typical in many others. So I'll describe my own. I'm one of a few thousand *emerging* American composers. The moniker suggests that our careers will eventually go somewhere, but that's unlikely in the current environment. I'm also an *independent* composer, which means that I'm not associated with a college or university. As an independent, I have very limited access to performance venues. I am, however, a member of a chamber ensemble, so I do have a few performance opportunities during each concert season. Each year, I enter about a dozen composition contests and respond to about a dozen calls for scores (A call for scores is an ensemble's published request for works to perform). Over the past decade, I've won five contests (two state, two national, one international), all of which resulted in prizes of between $100.00 and $600.00 and in single performances. During that same time I've received a dozen or so performances as the result of calls for scores and about three dozen performances through a combination of commissions, composer organization forums, festivals, and conferences, and my own chamber ensemble's concerts. All in all, during the past decade, I've received roughly 60 performances with audiences averaging about 100 people each. So about 6,000 people have heard live performances of something I've written. In addition, a few of my chamber pieces have received local airplay.

First performances of works, however well received, do not guarantee subsequent performances. Very few campus chamber music concerts are reviewed. And those reviews that are written are usually published in school newspapers and composer organization newsletters, so the general public doesn't see them.

I spend about 20 hours writing one minute of music, so a 10-minute piece takes me about 200 hours to write. If a piece is performed only twice and 100 people attend each performance, then I've invested an hour of labor for every listener's 10-minute exposure. Each package I send in response to a contest or call is costly, both in labor and in money. A typical package contains one or two photocopied scores, along with MIDI recording(s), and a self-addressed, stamped envelope for return of materials. We composers actually subsidize many contests via entry fees, which are typically about $15.00 to $30.00 per score. I'm one of a few hundred of the more successful American composers, in terms of contests and festival performances. But, during the 1990's, I spent about $10,000.00 and worked about 5,000 hours to earn a little over $3,000.00 (a net loss of $7,000.00) as a composer. So, for me, composition is basically just an expensive hobby.

It is extraordinarily frustrating to invest the effort and expense involved in writing music and submitting it to competitions. Why? Because while I'm preparing a submission, I know that it will probably be rejected and even if it is selected for performance, it will only be heard by a small group of people and may very well never be performed again. On the other hand, the infrequent successes are exhilarating.

When a critic remarks that there is little or nothing of value being written in this country, it is even more frustrating because I know that critics rarely attend such events. In general, I suspect that attending concerts involving works by the nameless rabble of the composition world is perceived as beneath their dignity or it just requires too much effort. Some critics probably aren't even aware that such events occur, but many others are probably too jaded to consider the possibility that they might actually hear something worthwhile. Having attended dozens of such performances over the past decade, however, I'm convinced that these concerts present most of the best new American chamber music.

Mainstream literary music shares common elements.

It occurs to me that I've explained more about what mainstream literary music *isn't* than about what it *is*. It isn't easily pigeonholed because it is not a single style or movement. It is more of an approach to the writing. Despite its diversity, it does have some common elements, though. Its practitioners have all carefully studied the craft of our predecessors. We've come to understand the significance of our heritage. Consequently, we don't casually cast aside the tools that Bach, Mozart, Berlioz, Brahms, Bartók, Debussy, Stravinsky, and many others have provided us. Barber and Copland, for example, were mainstream American literary composers. There are, in fact, thousands of us, but our names are largely unknown.

Mainstream literary composers seek to create works that deserve admission into the cumulative body of great concert literature. We're aware that gimmicks are cheap substitutes for real craft. We take care to assimilate the principles that have been amassed over the past several centuries so that we can contribute something of lasting value to the ongoing discourse. Over time, the art form has matured; there is more history to assimilate and less obvious space for meaningful contributions. Nonetheless, the gauntlet is ours to take up. And we do so willingly. Our music can be recognized by its preservation of traditional values like structural integrity, logical development of significant and audible patterns, and hierarchical dramatic shape.

THE GAUGE

One of my colleagues said that "quantifying quality" was an oxymoron. Actually, it's not. Quality is routinely quantified in manufacturing. For example, machine tools and engine parts are produced with flaws limited to $\pm n$ millionths of an inch; tires are warranted against defects in workmanship for a specified number of months or miles; cars are produced with mileage and emissions ratings. Foods and pharmaceutical products are assigned shelf lives and expiration dates. The FDA and USDA routinely inspect products in order to quantify quality by measuring purity in parts per million, by testing for bacteria and pesticides, by identifying unwanted additives. Buildings are constructed with indexing specifications that indicate levels of wind and earthquake resistance, insulation, and so forth. In sports, quality is quantified via player statistics (average points per game, no-hit innings pitched, runs batted in, world or conference ranking, etc.). Barry Bonds can be classified as a great batter based upon the quantification of his career. His statistics indicate a high degree of mastery in his profession. They don't tell us *why* he's able to do what he does; that requires much more specific data. But they are meaningful numbers nonetheless.

The postmodern argument that qualitative judgment is purely subjective is a seductive one. It's simple and straightforward. It requires no examination of the evidence—no discerning comparison of one work with another, no knowledge, no training, no insight. In short, once someone adopts this dogmatic view, he or she is permanently relieved of the need to exert the effort of thinking about the issue. Nonetheless, it's completely untrue.

In the preceding chapters about the musical brain and music history's progress paradigm, I presented some objectively verifiable indicators of quality in musical composition. Those who cling to the notion that qualitative judgment in the arts is a matter of opinion are unaware that composers make careful, deliberate decisions while writing—and that well-trained composers are equipped to make better decisions than poorly trained ones. I'm certain that many people would consider an objective gauge for measuring the quality of musical works offensive. Here are a few hypothetical arguments against formulating such a gauge followed by my responses:

- *A gauge would have a "chilling" effect on creativity because composers would be expected to write music that fits the gauge.* Right now, the inability of conductors and performers to locate good new music definitely *does* have a chilling effect because it leads them to rely on a combination of war-horses and inferior modern and postmodern works. If an objectively valid gauge can be implemented, then the only "chilling" effect will be a reduction in performances of inferior pieces.

- *A gauge could be used as an instrument for discriminating against genuine innovators whose work is valid but defies the criteria set forth in the gauge's standards.* The gauge should be subject to review and revision. If a work really is good but doesn't meet the gauge's criteria, then the gauge requires revision— but any revision should also specify objective standards. If there is something intrinsically good about a piece, it can be described in objective terms.

- *Art is and should remain fundamentally subjective. No objective standards can or should be formulated to evaluate it.* The *status quo*, which relies on subjectivity, doesn't work. At present, the music industry bases qualitative assessments on record sales (a flawed quantification of quality, but advantageous to the industry). Academia has an exclusive and self-perpetuating "old boy" network combined with an emphasis on ideology rather than craft (also flawed because it often bases qualitative judgment on extramusical factors like personal relationships, shared intellectual views, and mutual "back-scratching"). Government arts funding organizations base their judgment on social and political issues. The industry method is financially based and the academic and government approaches are politically, socially, and ideologically based. It would be far better for music if the criteria for judging it were musical.

Music's definition provides some criteria.

The last two words of music's definition *(biological rhythm)* are of critical importance in determining the musicality of a piece. We can readily categorize some "sound compositions" as either music or non-music. For example, silence alone does not represent biological rhythm. Nor do arrhythmic successions of essentially unrelated sounds. Furthermore, biological rhythm is hierarchical, so its representation is also hierarchical. Well-written music includes the following attributes:

- Microscopic events resemble short-term biological rhythm.
- Macroscopic structure is hierarchical, resembling long-term biological rhythm.
- Prominent material contains significant, non-habituating patterns.
- Textural components are integrated to serve a common rhythmic purpose.
- Strong thematic, dynamic, and textural contrasts clarify extended dramatic shape.
- Musical events unfold logically, imparting a sense of inevitability.

The Gestalt grouping principles provide some criteria.

For listeners to understand and predict events as they unfold, they must be able to perceive relationships among various components of the work's overall texture. So, music is *communicative* to the degree that it supports these Gestalt grouping principles:

- **Proximity:** Closer elements are grouped.
- **Similarity:** Similar elements are grouped.
- **Good Continuation:** Elements that follow each other in a given direction are grouped.
- **Common Fate:** Elements that change in the same way are grouped.
- **Familiarity:** Elements that we recognize are perceived as units.

So, for example, a pointillistic work that rapidly shifts the timbres and octave placements of melodic lines weakens the listener's predictive power because it violates the principles of grouping by similarity and good continuation.

Other psychological phenomena provide criteria.

In order for listeners to recognize and recall significant patterns, they should be conducive to the chunking process. This limits the duration of a single pattern to the perceptual present and also restricts the number of individual components it can contain. The law of affect reveals that delayed expectation enhances our emotional experience, so works that employ devices to delay expectations are more likely to be rewarding than those that do not. Both unity and contrast help us to recognize discrete events and, consequently, to structure our mental representations of significant patterns.

Recognition and predictive power are enhanced through grammatical consistency and precision. Every note serves a purpose and should be integrated within its context—vertically, horizontally, and motivically—so well that any substitution would weaken the passage. Consistency of grammar is important not only at the microscopic level but also at the macroscopic level. If, for example, one writes an "eclectic" work that vacillates among jazz, impressionistic, and Baroque styles, the audience's participation is hampered in much the same way that comprehension of a novel would be more difficult if some parts were written in Mark Twain's vernacular American style, some parts in Elizabethan English, and still other parts in modern French.

The progress paradigm provides additional criteria.

In order to advance the progress paradigm, a piece of music should be exploratory. Although it needn't be extraordinarily novel, it should avoid clichés and paradigm setbacks. New works modeled after music from the distant past (e.g., imitation-Renaissance) and other works that sacrifice history's "nuggets" represent setbacks. Works that offer gimmicks but neglect the fundamentals also represent setbacks to the paradigm regardless of how novel they might otherwise be.

Here are some sample evaluations based on the gauge.

Each musical excerpt in these samples is expository. That is, each represents the first occurrence of its content within a larger work. The first is my own. The second is the opening of Butch Rovan's *Antinomy*. The cryptic title is probably a misspelling of "antimony," which is a silvery white, brittle, metalic element *(L. stibium).*

Sample Evaluation 1

Location	Audible Content	Dramatic Shape
Clarinet Meas. 1-2	Meas. 1 motive (G-A-F) aurally chunked by accents, rests, and slurs. Congruous with meter. Proximity and good continuation. Immediate repetition for familiarity. Chunk size OK. Meas. 2 first E continues well from F. E-G-Eb suggest variation of Meas. 1 motive. Eb-D leap audibility is assisted by increased duration of D.	Meas. 1 motive provides a significant pattern, but exact repetition leaves hierarchical development temporarily ambiguous. Dynamics mp < f imply an increase in tension, as do staccatos in Meas. 2. 32nds raise pitch and increase pace, preparing for climax. Meas. 3. A is high, loud, long, and on strong beat, establishing unambiguous climax.
Hn, Cello Meas. 1-3	Cello line descends by whole step sequence. Good continuation and familiarity. Horns rise by half step sequence. Good continuation and familiarity. Share similarity of timbre, proximity, common fate. Delineated from cello by asynchrony, contrary and complementary motion (lack of common fate). Chunk size OK.	Texture is highly unified. Gradual spread of gap between cello and horns, combined with dynamics mp < f clearly increase tension. Increased density at Meas. 3 supports the clarinet climax. Both the cello and the horns present significant patterns.
Clarinet Meas. 3-4	Last 3 16ths of Meas. 3 suggest melodic contour from first beat of Meas. 2 (familiarity).	Sudden dynamic drop and softening of articulations on beat 2 of Meas. 3 imply beginning of descent from climax. Reversing the ascending M7 to form a descending m2 further decreases tension. Dynamic mp > and slower note values suggest point of repose.
Hn, Cello Meas. 3-4	Pattern of 3 16ths followed by a longer value suggest previous material (familiarity). Entire accompaniment shares common durations + articulations (similarity, common fate) and differs from melody (asynchronicity, lack of similarity and common fate).	Silence after first 16th of Meas. 3 supports clarinet descent. More fluid articulations begun in clarinet are continued in accompaniment. Shared dynamic mp > supports clarinet point of repose, as does slower pace.

General Observations: This scoring subject adheres well to gauge criteria. It has three clearly delineated textural components (melody, inner harmonic unit, and bass line). All three establish and maintain audible patterns to facilitate the listener's predictive power. Each is assigned a single timbre for clarity. The upper line confirms its prominence in the second measure by pursuing the most varied course within the context. The inner harmonic unit (horns) begins as a syncopated harmonic/rhythmic figure that ascends chromatically and maintains its identity through the climax. The bass line (cello) maintains its character as well. All three components support a common rhythmic goal. The dynamic markings, which apply to all parts, are also congruous with that goal. Evidence of the overall hierarchical structure is quite clear. Smaller components (e.g., the chunks in the melody) are grouped into larger ones. In addition, articulations differentiate functions of increased and decreased tension (meas 1-3 vs. meas 3-4). An untrained listener's attention will naturally gravitate to the upper line because it is the most varied and will be apprehended as the most "interesting." A more astute listener may manage to establish aural expectations regarding the progress of all three components. And an expert listener may notice that the clarinet and cello lines are motivically related, that the middle lines move in parallel fourths, and that the general harmonic implications are quartal.

Sample Evaluation 2

Location	Audible Content	Dramatic Shape
Clarinet Meas. 1-2	Although the opening triplet figure passes rapidly with large leaps, its melodic contour is quite distinct and conducive to chunking. The high C/Db syncopations establish an audibly significant pattern, although its repetitions are too varied to formulate predictions.	The opening phrase rises quickly to a series of repeated notes characterized by syncopation. The second high Db (accented) is climactic and the final C suggests a bit of a return toward repose.
Piano Meas. 2	The quintuplet 16ths appear on beat 1, helping to establish meter. Their melodic contour is distinct, although specific pitches will not likely be assimilated because it is very disjunct and the number of notes struck per 16th varies. The recurring pattern of a 32nd followed by a tied note is significant and clearly reinforces the earlier clarinet figure, but the irregularity with which it recurs prohibits the formulation of expectations.	The accented and tied A ending the quintuplet 16ths suggests a climax, but its location contradicts that of the clarinet's climax, so the two parts are somewhat uncoordinated. The bass clef pairs that follow (C-B and C-Bb) further weaken the piano part at the moment the clarinet climax is reached. As the clarinet settles toward repose, the piano ascends to a new climax (high Eb).
Clarinet Meas. 2-4	The low F serves to sustain. Its significance is elevated by the decrescendo and crescendo and it is easily chunked. The final 3 notes form an audible melodic contour, but the relationship between the high E and the low D is not likely to be heard. Because the meter is very weak, the triplet is likely to be heard as ambiguously varied note values.	The decrescendo and crescendo on F help to reduce and then increase tension, leading to the second climax on E.
Piano Meas. 3-4	The triplet figure in Meas 3 is distinct, but its placement on the second half of the second beat after no previous attacks in the measure is metrically ambiguous. The rhythmic relationship between it and the syncopated low D and high Gb that follow will be heard but not the pitch relationships. The final left-hand 16ths of Meas 3 and the B on beat 1of Meas 4 help to establish meter somewhat, but not enough to support the offbeats that follow in the right hand. The doubly-dotted 8ths in particular will be heard as mis-timed quarters on beat 2. Since the left hand B crosses between the right hand high Gb and the right hand diads that follow, the listener will likely associate the Gb with the B followed by the right hand's Bb and simultaneously maintain the Eb-Bb pickup relationship to B, so salient information will probably be lost.	The high Gb in Meas 3 suggests a point of stress, but it is not well prepared by the preceding left hand triplet figure. The sparse texture (left hand low D and the clarinet's sustained F) tend to weaken its significance as a climax. The A-C diad in Meas. 4 is accented, implying a point of stress, but there is no preparation or resolution to support that role. The Eb-Bb diad do little to support the clarinet's climax or to establish any dramatic meaning.

General Observations: This scoring subject does not adhere well to gauge criteria. The passage contains several potentially significant patterns but there is little indication that they will be developed or even repeated. There is very little evidence of continuity—that is, the significant patterns that do exist seem discrete (except for the 32nds followed by tied notes), so it is difficult to associate consecutive events for storage and retrieval. The sense of meter is weak. As a result, the durations will not be cataloged readily because they lack a frame of reference. There are some hints at dramatic shape, but they're all ambiguous. This passage almost completely deprives the listener of any predictive power or meaningful reflection as events unfold, so the audience cannot vicariously participate in the composition process. Either it will engender intellectual frustration or it will be apprehended on the sensuous plane alone.

This gauge serves as a point of departure.

The gauge that I've presented is both objective and effective—at least for comparing works that vary significantly in quality—but it is rudimentary. For brevity's sake, I've evaluated very short excerpts, but this presentation should suffice to demonstrate that quantification of quality is indeed possible, even in the arts. The principles I've presented here can be applied to development as well as exposition. My gauge's usefulness should become more apparent still when the relative merits of several complete works are compared based on its criteria. That is, many pieces adhere to the gauge, but some do so more effectively than others.

The gauge as it stands can differentiate between works that have significant patterns and those that don't and between those that have audible dramatic shape and those that don't. It can readily rank works that vary significantly in quality. I have not refined it to include all objectively verifiable factors. There are, for example, works that have dramatic shape but lack finesse in imparting a sense of inevitability. Ultimately, it should be feasible to refine the gauge until virtually any two works can be fairly compared and ranked, but that will take time and research.

The gauge as I've presented it lacks subtlety, but there are many more areas that will probably find objective confirmation in time. For example, during the common practice era, a convention similar to *musica ficta* arose in the management of melodic patterns in minor keys. The melodic minor scale included raised 6th and 7th degrees during ascent and unaltered 6th and 7th degrees during descent. This established strong expectations about melodic direction. I'm not suggesting that the common practice era offered the best possible approach to melody, but I do believe that the musical context at a given moment establishes expectations that transcend acculturation. Another technique worth investigating is the convention of introducing the most significant material in the highest and lowest parts (usually the highest—as one might expect based on Diana Deutsch's "scale illusion" research). Composers are intuitively aware that this enhances the audibility of significant patterns by presenting them as outlines or borders of the overall texture. On those occasions when significant material is introduced in the inner parts it is generally reinforced to gain prominence through sheer volume. These techniques and many others merit empirical study by psychologists.

Because the gauge is incomplete, composers who understand and concur with its implications and who have, themselves, assimilated the progress paradigm should be the first to put it into practice. When two or more works are similarly evaluated by my sketchy criteria, the careful consideration of structural details should reveal further objectively measurable discrepancies between them. But the process of refinement should be reviewed to insure that it doesn't become arbitrary or subjective.

The implementation, exercise, and review of such a gauge should naturally make it more subtle and robust over time. Applicable psychological research is ongoing and should be incorporated as findings become available. There is potential for such a gauge to be abused, of course, but that potential is minimal so long as the people who refine it rely upon objectively verifiable criteria rather than personal stylistic preferences. The modern and postmodern mistakes are certainly grave enough to justify corrective action of some kind, so at worst, using this gauge would be better than maintaining the *status quo.*

Incidentally, variants of the principles used here probably apply to the other arts as well, because many of the same psychological principles apply to sensory input in general. For example, a Jackson Pollack painting would probably score poorly using a similar visually-oriented gauge because his work relies excessively upon unity without variety (habituating and inhibiting to significant pattern recognition) and exposition without development (lack of dramatic shape).

CHANGING PRIORITIES

Extramusical interference should cease.

By now, this should be obvious, but accomplishing it will require some tough-minded scrutiny of the current state of concert music. Performers play a key role in the solution because they determine what gets programmed. Performers must begin to play more new music and must also engage their minds when selecting new literature. But performers have now become accustomed to the 20th Century tradition of studying the war-horses in school and of being evaluated based on their ability to "interpret" the war-horses (meaning basically to duplicate the time-honored interpretations that have been handed down to them by their teachers).

I don't advocate discontinuing this process, but it should be balanced with the need to grow by learning new literature. At least 50% of music performed should be new. 60% would be better still. A century ago, nearly everything that was performed was new. Now, only a relatively small number of performers have carved out niches by specializing in new music. It would be better if all performers were taught to regard new music performance as critical. They should learn to seek out new music that they can play with conviction—music that engages their minds by providing meaningful dramatic shape and audible structure. They shouldn't be swayed by dollar signs or composer reputations. Rather, they should play music they believe is worth playing.

Because the *avant-garde* became the *status-quo* for new music during the second half of the 20th Century, chamber music performers who specialize in new music have introduced a new problem: the ghettoizing of

189

new literature. That is, they perform concerts that are devoted entirely to music that is characterized as "adventuresome" or "exploratory," and thus isolate new literature from mainstream venues. Much of it requires extraordinary facility—for example, the use of multiphonics for wind players, extremely complex counting tasks, and so forth, so it provides a showcase for very highly skilled players to demonstrate their remarkable virtuosity. Result: New music specialists now have a great deal of effort and reputation invested in performances of music that violates the progress paradigm and audiences have come to associate "new" with "strange and difficult" or even "annoying". Actually, it's no longer adventuresome to perform what is now traditional anyway.

This modernist performance practice has led to an analogous postmodernist practice as well. There are now groups who issue calls for chamber music scores that are specifically influenced by jazz, folk music, and "world music"—a sort of musical role reversal. Popular styles have been enhanced over the past few centuries because they've been influenced by mainstream literary music, not *vice versa*. This is as it should be because folk and popular styles haven't adopted the entire progress paradigm. Without the influence of mainstream literary music, popular music would still be short, stilted, and monophonic. Although there are significant works that borrow material from the popular vernacular (e.g., the music of Ives and Copland), such material must be handled with great care. Furthermore, these works have properly represented the exception rather than the rule. If ensembles come to perceive such music as the core of new literature, then composers will be coerced into writing it simply because they can't otherwise expect their music to be performed.

The lack of performance opportunities for new mainstream literature is exacerbated by the fact that most of it is either unpublished or self-published. This, of course, makes it very difficult to find. But various resources, including the internet, are beginning to change this. In addition to my "day job" as a senior computer programmer for Unisys, I'm webmaster for the National Association of Composers, USA (NACUSA) and the Composer-Conductor Bridge. Here are URLs for those sites and a few others that list concert works (modernist, postmodernist, and mainstream) by living Americans:

American Music Center:
WWW.AMC.NET
American Society of Composers, Authors, and Publishers (ASCAP):
ASCAP.COM
Center for Promotion of Contemporary Composers:
WWW.UNDER.ORG/CPCC/
Composer-Conductor Bridge:
WWW.MUSIC-USA.ORG/CCBRIDGE/
National Association of Composers, USA (NACUSA):
WWW.MUSIC-USA.ORG/NACUSA/

Government funding for new music should increase.

The war-horse mentality needn't continue. When invited to do so, audiences are still capable of understanding and enjoying new works, even though the music may offer challenges. Clinton Nieweg, Principal Librarian of the Philadelphia Orchestra recently wrote the following:

> After listening intently as The Philadelphia Orchestra performed three new compositions by three emerging composers, the attending audience completed ballots at intermission to help choose the winning work in the Orchestra's Centennial Composition Competition…."The atmosphere at intermission throughout the Academy of Music, as people discussed their choices, was quite remarkable to witness. From the comments people wrote on their ballots it is absolutely clear how much the audience enjoyed being involved. It was obvious from the extraordinary sense of attention during the performances that everyone was listening, reacting to, and thinking about each of these three very different pieces before choosing one over another."…Gurewitsch notes that the audience

"seemed conspicuously less gray than usual," since blocks of tickets were offered to music schools. Music Director Wolfgang Sawallisch noted "the enthusiasm with which the audience had greeted the unfamiliar composers."[37]

This shows that audiences are receptive to new works—that the failed war-horse, "pops," and ghettoizing strategies aren't necessary. Indeed, new mainstream literary works belong in exactly the same venues as their older counterparts.

In standard business fashion, the popular music industry is attempting to eliminate its competitors, which include literary music. Consider the following observation by Donald Erb:

> The music industry is in the hands of businessmen and accountants who haven't the faintest idea about anything musical. They are only interested in destroying the competition. Twenty some years ago, non-pop music represented 20% of the record market. Today the figure is more like 2%. Much of that is, in my opinion, by design. There is very little interest on the part of most classical record companies in recording anything except that which they feel will make a profit. What little profit which was made in recording the same standard works over and over is now gone.[38]

Literary music—including the war-horses—doesn't generate sufficient revenue to support itself. It never has. This is the main reason that the U.S. government wisely established the National Endowment for the Arts. But that organization is grossly under-funded and continually threatened with further cuts. Even before the recent NEA cuts, public arts funding in the U.S. was vastly lower than its counterparts in the other industrialized nations. Nonetheless, according to Newt Gingrich, the fact that the arts generate so little revenue is grounds for abolishing the NEA altogether. That is, if the arts can't pay for themselves, then people don't want them and, therefore, apparently don't need them. His solution is to have the artists themselves subsidize the arts:

> If the people who come to lobby us who are famous and rich dedicate one percent of their gross incomes to an American endowment for the arts, they would fund a bigger system than the national endowment funds.[39]

Gingrich obviously doesn't realize that the rich people who lobby Congress are mostly members of the entertainment industry. Very few representatives of high art are financially above middle class and many would be destitute if we quit our "day jobs."

William F. Buckley, Jr., a genuine blue-blooded American *elitist,* feels that the arts should be funded, but that only established works should receive support. His attitude is that of the aristocrat who has no real knowledge either of music or of the issues confronting musicians. His article endorsing funding is, in reality, a thinly veiled rationale for stifling the creation of new works:

> The National Endowment for the Arts should be given a fresh mandate, to continue to make grants—but only to qualified symphony orchestras, ballet and opera companies, and museums to help pay the cost of bringing to the public acknowledged classics in art created fifty or more years ago. That test of longevity does not demean artistic work created yesterday, but acknowledges that the passage of time has also the critical effect of seasoned validation.[40]

This plan would force financially troubled ensembles (i.e., practically everybody) to completely abandon the performance of new music. Who would have supported the acknowledged masters of the past if this approach had been taken? In the absence of financial support, the art from fifty years ago would never have been presented to the public. Therefore, it would have gained no recognition. If art is not seen or heard in its own time, how does it gain recognition later? The art that represents our culture is the art of the present, not of the past. Buckley's plan would effectively ban music by living composers with the untenable claim that it would somehow miraculously gain recognition 50 years hence without the benefit of performance.

If the Buckley plan were adopted, "unqualified" but *developing* organizations that, with some nurturing, might eventually qualify would be cut off. Consequently, they would wither and die. If we applied Buckley's approach to science, we would eliminate all funding for new research. We would dedicate our money to the process of reprinting and disseminating the time-tested scientific advances of 50 or more years ago.

By Buckley's definition, the monuments of our society are actually the monuments of our ancestors. The great works of the past should, of course, be preserved and performed. And they're not in imminent danger in this regard. Most new works, however, are never recorded because there are no funds available to record them. Many are never even performed. As a consequence, most living composers are very poorly compensated, so we earn our livings by other means, so we have little time to devote to writing. Although past masterpieces are in almost no danger, the music of living composers is in constant danger—not just of failing to be preserved and performed, but of failing to be written at all. Arts funding does involve risk, to be sure. But if we fail to take the risk that we might occasionally create something of no lasting value, we also risk failing to create anything at all. Considerably more money, not less, should be earmarked for the *creation* of new art. Do we measure the greatness of past cultures by their ability to preserve art from the even more ancient past? No. We measure their greatness by the art they *created*.

Artistic rather than political standards should be applied.

It all begins with the money. Like it or not, how the government's money is spent reveals its real priorities. Right now, a great deal of NEA money is being spent on "cultural diversity." Ensembles must have boards of directors with the right ethnic and gender mix. They must also take such factors into account when submitting grant proposals. Consequently, quality of programming content is often a secondary consideration. Before American concert music can get back on track, this must change. I'm not at all suggesting that only white men should write music. Quite the contrary. I'm saying that race, gender, and sexual orientation have absolutely nothing to do with the quality of a composer's work and, therefore, should have absolutely nothing to do with the selection process either.

It would not be difficult to establish a committee to evaluate submissions of music from all American composers. The NEA could publish an annual open call for scores. There would probably be fewer than 3,000 entrants. Works could be judged and composers could be ranked based on specific and objective criteria such as those I provided in the "gauge" chapter. It would serve no purpose to evaluate musical works based on name recognition, popularity, or record sales because many of the currently recognized composers—especially among the postmodernists—are actually not very good. The modernist "old boy" network has many people with extremely impressive credentials who simply don't write well. The only satisfactory way to circumvent such pitfalls is to require anonymous submission. After ranking, composers should receive feedback regarding where we rank and why and we should be able to resubmit works annually.

Money is tight. Only deserving composers should be funded to write. Right now, ensembles are motivated by financial distress to commission the "stars" and the "well knowns" in hopes of securing strong concert attendance. The NEA could publish a ranked listing of composers that prospective commissioning groups could consult. They could also establish an official certification process that prohibits the funding of unranked composers. Bad works by well-known composers would no longer be so desirable. Suddenly, ensembles would stop commissioning shoddy works because the federal government wouldn't reimburse them. The result would be quite an "eye-opener" for the NEA, for ensembles, and for the concert-going public. And the NEA would get a political bonus thrown in: They wouldn't have to explain to Congress why they paid $80,000.00 for the creation of a worthless piece of junk.

Teaching credentials should reflect real artistic standards.

Composition prizes and publication in music journals significantly impact the viability of a composition teacher's career. But many bad composers have received prizes for vapid novelty and they've published articles that don't represent artistic or intellectual excellence because they're based on faulty assumptions. Many such people are currently training students to follow in their footsteps. Music theory departments should carefully review their teaching methods with an eye toward reestablishing the main-stream literary model. This should not present a major hardship. On the whole, even those composition teachers who've made the modern and postmodern mistakes in their own work have strong training in traditional music theory. If they're to teach composition and not just music theory, however, they should be expected to *prove* that they can write well. All composers are music theorists but not all music theorists are composers—regardless of their training. My NEA ranking and certification scheme should be useful in this regard.

Music critics should have strong music credentials.

The cycle of mastery has important implications regarding the field of music criticism. If a critic is not himself an accomplished performer, then his ability to judge performances is greatly impaired because he has not assimilated the performer's knowledge of the progress paradigm. And if he's not a thoroughly trained composer, then his ability to judge new music is similarly impaired because he cannot reasonably expect to recognize an effective new course for the paradigm. This explains why so many past critiques are now held up for ridicule. But many critics—egotistically certain of their superior listening skills—continue to assert ignorant opinions as facts. Historically, arts patrons relied upon the advice of elder masters to identify promising young composers. It was a wise system. Now critics largely determine whose music is worthy, despite the fact that there is no standard for certifying critics. At present, the only prerequisites for the job are the ability to write at a fourth grade level and the desire to express opinions. Musically unschooled journalists who say, "I don't know art, but I know what I like" should seek work elsewhere.

Critics should first be professional musicians—a logical conclusion, but one that is sure to meet with some well-prepared defensive rhetoric. Actually, working musicians *are* often hired to work as part time or free-lance critics. This is a particularly good strategy for several reasons. First, each can review that which most closely resembles his or her specialty. A pianist can review piano recitals, a conductor can review large ensemble concerts, a composer can review new works, and so forth. Second, critics who work locally as musicians are likely to have a better understanding of the community's musical needs. Third, in this arrangement, the community gets to hear the critics themselves at work, so their personal musical skills are likely to influence the weight attributed to their opinions—which is just and proper. Fourth, musician-critics who are subject to review are more likely to exercise empathy when contemplating negative reviews. Fifth, many very fine musicians are under-employed. The additional part-time work might enable a good player to stay in the area and keep playing. Sixth, critics should, above all, be *advocates* for literary music—something which comes naturally to musicians. Persuading people to attend even mediocre concerts is better than discouraging them from coming. The fact is, most people don't really know how good the players are until somebody else tells them. They're impressed that the people on stage can read music and memorize lots of notes and move their fingers quickly and play more or less in tune and together. If literary music is to survive, audiences must be built, not torn down.

Music commentary should facilitate effective listening.

This principle applies to music commentary in general, not just to new music, but it is especially important with new music. As I've already mentioned, concentrating on the composer's personal life provides no assistance to listeners. When presenting an unfamiliar piece, even an amateur musician with modest analytical skills can give listeners some audible features to listen for. The commentary needn't be profound, but it should draw the audience's attention to the music itself. Depending upon the piece, it might be useful to discuss the basic materials (harmonic content, scales used, chromaticism, polytonality), applicable textures (polyphony, homophony, heterophony), important structural features (where the themes appear), methods used to develop the material (imitative counterpoint, augmentation, inversion), instrumentation (electronics, special effects), and so forth. Pertinent information can often be gleaned from record jacket notes and music appreciation textbooks.

Media executives should set the tone.

Elvis Presley has been sighted more since his death than Jesus was. As the 25th anniversary of Elvis's death approached, CNN ran a piece about a "psychic" whose plaster statue of Elvis purportedly sheds tears. They showed the statue, of course, and presented the story as though it were legitimate news. If the guy really believed that he had regular conversations with Elvis, then the story would have been a disgraceful exploitation of his mental illness. But the statue's "tears" reveal that he's simply a fraud. If he was unable to earn a living by bilking gullible people before the broadcast, he will probably be able to do so with CNN's help. Why would a highly respected news source share his hoax as though it were legitimate news? For the ratings, of course. This sort of yellow journalism should be beneath even those who mistakenly believe that "the king" was a great "artist."

Media chains are, of course, motivated to increase their profits, so they're naturally attracted to strategies that boost subscription sales and broadcast ratings. Nonetheless, they should rediscover the distinction between marketing and journalism. Media editors, publishers, and station managers hire critics and commentators. They also determine layouts, program formats, and so forth. Promotional material should be segregated from news and commentary. Many newspapers, for example, carry entertainment inserts that begin with large color pictorial spreads—often overflowing with ludicrous hyperbole about the "great" rock band that's coming to town or the "blockbuster" movie that's opening this weekend. After all of the hype, there are a few short two-sentence blurbs about other events. *Real* reviews should be up front. Paid advertisements should be in the back and should be clearly labeled as such. TV news programs routinely present music industry marketing propaganda as though it is news. Musically illiterate rock stars are regularly interviewed—as though their profound insights will enlighten us. Journalists should be journalists, not entertainers. They should seek real news stories and leave the hype to advertisers.

Public school music study should be regarded as essential.

Music is primarily an intuitive activity. We exercise the same pattern-recognition principles when listening to it that our ancestors used for survival. When we hear what could be a meaningful pattern, our intuition alerts us. We then begin verbal-analytical reflection. We listen more intently. If a pattern recurs, we concentrate harder still—struggling to identify its source and specific character, just as one might struggle to discern whether the leaves rustled because of a stalking predator or just the wind. If there's no discernable pattern or the source is mundane, we turn our attention elsewhere. If the pattern is monotonous, we become habituated to it and our attention wanders again. What we're really looking for is *significant* patterns. A well-crafted piece of music is fraught with multi-leveled and intricate patterns of considerable significance. It's "food for thought" to the intuitive mode.

When attentive non-linguistic listening is engendered, our intuition is called to action. We become aware of subtle patterns. But there's not often a life-and-death need for intuitive thinking in our daily lives anymore, so the intuitive mode doesn't often get the exercise it needs to develop. Most people are not routinely engaged in creative work or scientific speculation. In the absence of the old need—the real-time survival need—we have allowed the intuitive mode to lapse into a state of relative disuse. But we still need intuitive thinkers—now more than ever. Humanity currently faces a plethora of problems that are both vast and tremendously complex. If solutions are forthcoming, they will originate in intuitive thought. I don't believe there's a better intuition exercise than the study of music. And I'm not talking about that shallow business of listening to somebody else play a Mozart piece for fifteen minutes immediately before you take a test. I'm talking about the whole enchilada—music lessons throughout childhood. Current brain research makes it quite clear that mental stimulation promotes brain development.

Active physical participation in music is more immediate and intense than passive listening. Playing a musical instrument calls into use not only the pattern-recognition process, but also the connections between the brain and the body. It engages the musician in a complex feedback loop: A finger presses a key. The hearing apparatus translates an aural stimulus into a mental signal. The brain decides instantly whether you're playing the right note, whether it's in tune and whether it is correct in volume. If it's flat or sharp, your lips or larynx make a fine pitch adjustment. If it's too loud or soft, your diaphragm makes an adjustment in pressure applied to the lungs. Your intuition works with your verbal-analytical mode to decide whether the current passage fits properly within the musical context. With time and training, musicians can develop skills that are remarkably refined and subtle. This is a kind of non-verbal thinking that should not be mistaken for illogical. It is actually quite precise, although it can be difficult to verbalize. Music teachers frequently resort to communicating by example ("Play it like this…") because describing the objective verbally is tedious, time-consuming, and often ineffective. Nonetheless, the desired effect is quite tangible. Audiences tend to be impressed by instrumental performers who demonstrate virtuosity through speed. It is inconceivable to our verbal-analytical minds that a concert pianist can so rapidly process all the information required to play a wonderfully even passage of ascending parallel sixths in thirty-second notes in her right hand while her left hand plays descending octaves in eighth-note triplets.

In the creative mind, the two modes make a coordinated effort. The intuitive mode offers a "hunch" which the verbal-analytical mode reflects upon. Music stimulates and exercises our intuition, making it more effective in its respective role. Key words like *hunch* and *inspiration* are verbal-analytical descriptions of intuitive activities. The fact that many people think of *inspiration* (literally "breathing in") as a gift from God—that it involves an illumination from a source outside our own minds—shows just how out of touch our verbal-analytical and intuitive modes are.

So what? I work both as a musician and as a computer programmer. I've often heard the statement that musicians make good programmers. Software companies have even published employment ads stipulating that applicants should either be proficient in a specific programming language or be *musicians*. This was going on long before the "Mozart Effect" was made public, by the way. I also suspect that if people working in math and science were surveyed about their childhood experiences, we would discover that an inordinately high number of them took music lessons.

Music curricula should emphasize mainstream literary music.

How we behave as adults is significantly shaped by what we learn during our years in school. Kids who learn that rock and roll is the best music there is usually become adults who maintain that opinion. Consequently, they don't often seek opportunities to continue growing and learning about music. Adults who have had a modicum of musical training can gain lifelong satisfaction from it by participating in community ensembles and by attending public concerts. Active participation in such intellectual pursuits is essential for brain development. When budgets are tight, this is seen as a "frill" issue, but it's really much more. The pace of change is accelerating. The typical American adult will experience a career that spans several different occupations, so we must come to understand education as an ongoing proposition. To be adaptable, we need to exercise our brains.

> Industrial music, which is also known as "noise", and other new styles of music are worthy of study in our schools and consideration by our scholars and intellectuals. This study may provide a way to bridge the generation gap between students and teachers, as well as the philosophical gap between intellectuals, such as musicologists and theorists, and the public-at-large. Also, it may provide a means of gaining insight into how the world has changed and some of the roles music plays in it. This bridging and understanding would help gain financial support from and foster intellectual curiosity in the society-at-large.[41]

Sheldon Atovsky's position in the paragraph above is predicated on the assumption that all opinions are equal—that the discrepancy between a teacher's *informed* opinion and a student's *uninformed* opinion is merely a matter of cultural bias. Is it the responsibility of the teacher to "bridge the generation gap" by tacitly acknowledging the validity of the student's opinions? Is it the teacher's responsibility to gain financial support from "society-at-large" by acquiescence? Couldn't it be that the teacher, through years of concentrated study, has learned something that the students and the society-at-large haven't?

I agree with part of the following, but not with Atovsky's intended implications. Atovsky's suggestion of an "egalitarian respect for the wide spectrum of even contradictory ideas and opinions" represents the mistaken postmodern assertion that all opinions are equal:

> The strong impact of such easy and quick access to so much information has led to changes of attitudes in segments of the population. Two of these changes are the increased questioning of the superiority of traditional points of view over those that are less traditional and the development of a more egalitarian respect for the wide spectrum of even contradictory ideas and opinions inherent to the abundant information and knowledge available. The latter is due especially to the present situation in which the amount of available information on virtually any subject is so overwhelming that one's regular life style does not allow for the time necessary to carefully evaluate all of it. Consequently the value of some category, A, of a particular subject when compared to the value of another category, B, of the same subject, may be of arbitrarily equal or even superior worth due more to the fact that A has been considered and that B has not.[41]

I agree with Atovsky's observation that there has been "increased questioning of the superiority of traditional points of view," but questions alone do not automatically invalidate traditional music curricula. His mistaken assumption about categories A (literary music) and B (popular music) is that seriously trained musicians have not been sufficiently exposed to popular music to form meaningful opinions about it. Popular music is ubiquitous. It plays constantly on television and radio, in supermarkets, restaurants, movie soundtracks, and so forth. Furthermore, most American popular music is harmonically and melodically rooted in European common practice, so trained musicians can easily grasp its grammar. Familiarity is the foremost reason it's popular.

Literary music is taken seriously in *academia* because it is structurally superior to popular music. Analysis of mainstream literary masterpieces yields evidence of remarkable structural integrity, clarity of purpose, thorough and logical development, subtlety, ingenuity, and profound depth. Analysis of most popular music reveals that it is riddled with *clichés* and much weaker in direction and development than most literary music.

The postsecondary academic establishment has been unduly influenced by both modernism and postmodernism. Composition students should be discouraged from emulating both modernist and postmodernist doctrines. Our music schools shouldn't acquiesce to postmodern pressures by initiating programs in popular idioms. Although it is a hard pill to swallow, composition teachers should teach techniques that are verifiably musical. Reputations and money are at stake, so changing the *status quo* is a difficult proposition, but it is also a critical one. Current composition teachers have been thoroughly trained in music theory, so they don't need remedial instruction in order to change curricula, but they do need a change of mindset. The progress paradigm survived into the 20th Century in the works of composers like Debussy, Stravinsky, Bartók, Ravel, and Hindemith. It is also well represented by Americans like Barber, Copland, and Bernstein. These people produced a remarkable legacy for student composers to emulate, whereas most mid-century modernist "innovations" should be regarded as giant steps backward.

Colleges and Universities have begun to abandon hard-won academic freedoms by introducing curricula that conform to the new political agenda. Music history, literature, and appreciation textbooks are being revised to include chapters on rock, rap, world music, and so forth. Minimalist and New Age composers figure heavily in accounts of current concert music trends. New textbooks bear titles like *Understanding Popular Music* and *Rap Music and the Poetics of Identity.* The "new analysis" replaces the study of musical works themselves with the study of extramusical factors like the social, political, ethnic, and historical contexts in which pieces were written. This approach is likely to misdirect student composers toward the inferior but palatable dogma of cultural relativism. Students can avoid grappling with the great intellectual challenges that history's master composers have entrusted to us. Unfettered by the truth—that craft is of paramount importance in composition—they can learn that "anything goes"—that whatever they write is just as valid as anything else ever written. The students don't know any better; they only know what they're taught. But what excuses can our institutions of higher learning offer? We didn't want to offend anybody? We just gave them what they wanted? We did it for the money?

AFTERWORD

Like Sir Isaac Newton, I, too, am standing on the shoulders of giants. Writing this book has been the best composition lesson I've ever had. Like many composers of my generation, my personal journey has been from the aurally obfuscating principles of modernism toward the straightforward and clear principles of mainstream literary music. Most of the music I wrote during the 70's and 80's was highly structured, but its structure was largely based on modernist techniques because I was trying to emulate the work of my immediate predecessors. I *was* a modernist and, consequently, the act of composing was a struggle. I was routinely dissatisfied with my inability to achieve musically satisfying results. With few performance opportunities, I seldom actually got to hear my work to determine what was wrong.

Even so, I was intuitively headed in the right direction—clarifying the architecture—strengthening contrasts, and so forth—especially coordinating textural components and leaving "white space" where applicable. But my progress was slow. Consequently, with only a couple of exceptions, my catalog begins in 1990. My progress was slow because I hadn't yet discovered the connections between music history and the Gestalt principles. Verbal-analytical mode theorizing still overly influenced my work. Based on conversations with other composers, my experience of a 20-year setback seems typical. Now, armed with new knowledge, I'm eager to revisit some of my own music to apply the lessons I've learned while writing this book.

It's time to set the record straight. There are many powerful and well-connected people who will likely find this book offensive (assuming that they read it). Postmodernists in the music industry will probably accuse me of elitism or Euro-centricity. Modernists in the academic establishment will claim that I simply don't understand the significance of their work. Both groups have a great deal of time and labor invested in their respective positions. But they're wrong nonetheless. Here's why in a nutshell:

- Music is not simply "organized sound" as some modernists have proposed. It is the use of sound to represent biological rhythm. As such, it is audibly rhythmic and hierarchical.
- By extending the concept of elders, music notation enabled European composers to advance the art of music. This is not, as postmodernists would claim, a "culturally biased" assertion. It is a demonstrable fact.
- The survival potential for a musical innovation is increased if it either enhances music's ability to represent biological rhythm or increases its efficiency in communicating.
- Concert music communicates by enabling listeners to participate vicariously in the act of composition. Composers must provide significant audible patterns and logical development that is conducive to prediction and meaningful reflection in order to engage audiences.
- The Gestalt grouping principles and other psychological factors supply objective information for evaluating music's communicability.
- Composers who fail to assimilate the accumulated wisdom of their predecessors also fail to contribute to music's development.
- Verbal-analytical modernist composition systems represent a step backward because they reduce communicability.
- Simplistic postmodern styles represent a major step backward both in communicability and in the representation of biological rhythm.
- The extramusical factors that have influenced modernism and postmodernism are detrimental to long-term musical progress and, therefore, should be curtailed.

- New music that adheres to the mainstream literary tradition should recover its place in American concert halls. Achieving this requires changes in government funding guidelines and in the fields of music education and criticism.

My aim hasn't been to offend anybody, although I'm sure I have. It's unavoidable when dealing honestly with so controversial a topic. But if this book helps some composers avoid the modern and postmodern mistakes, then it will have served its purpose. The future of concert music is at stake. I'm just one of thousands of underrepresented mainstream literary composers. I'm not the Mozart of the 21st Century. I probably won't even achieve the stature of a Salieri. But someone among us very likely *is* the Mozart of the 21st Century. Since there are more well-schooled composers now than ever before, I'm quite confident that there are several great composers living at this moment, but we'll never know who they are until their music is heard. Right now, a mainstream literary composer's chance of getting the performances he or she deserves is on a par with winning the lottery. This book should help to change that by bringing an element of objectivity to the discourse. The gauge I've presented is the *Rosetta Stone*—albeit unpolished—for identifying musical works of quality. There is simply no better explanation for the evidence.

I've painted this book with a broad brush. I've addressed very general issues because they needed addressing and they're far more important than the details. For example, discovering the fundamental errors in John Cage's approach to composition is more useful than determining exactly why he chose note X in measure Y of piece Z. In fact, once you understand what's wrong with his approach, you'll realize that there's no point in studying his music at all. Any theorist who reads this book and agrees with me will find plenty of gaps to fill in between my broad strokes. And any theorist who disagrees will find plenty of uncrossed T's and undotted I's to criticize. But I doubt that anybody will uncover a fundamental flaw in my argument.

Here is my advice to my fellow composers: As I mentioned earlier, the pioneers of modernism provided us with many pregnant alternatives to pursue. I believe that the best course of action now is to revisit the music of Bartók, Stravinsky, Prokofiev, Poulenc, Debussy, and other early modernists and then pick up where they left off. At the beginning of the 20th Century, many composers abandoned common practice more or less simultaneously because it offered no unexploited resources. Nonetheless, most of them managed to preserve the fundamentals by adhering to the Gestalt principles, chunking judiciously, and so forth. Regardless of whether you backtrack or forge ahead, you should attend to the fundamentals.

I'm not the "style police." I believe it's *possible* to write effectively in any style you damned well please (although I haven't personally encountered a convincing crossover or minimalist work). Concert music is intended to communicate with an audience. Whether you write "uptown" music based on mathematical constructs or "downtown" music based on the *I Ching,* extramusical formulae tend to interfere with assimilation and prediction. Regardless of how novel or colorful or theoretically intriguing your system may be, audiences will be unable to participate vicariously in the act of composition *unless you take special care to insure that the significant patterns in your work are audible.* If you're a minimalist or a New Age composer, then your work—regardless of how audible it may be—represents a setback *unless you take special care to present significant patterns and to develop your material.* If you're a "new tonalist" or a quasi-common-practice "melodist," then your work represents a setback, *unless you take special care to bring something original to the discourse.*

ABOUT THE AUTHOR

John Winsor studied clarinet with Robert Harrison, David Harris, and Robert Marcellus of the Cleveland Orchestra and composition with John Rinehart and James Waters. He received a Bachelor of Music degree from Heidelberg College and a Master of Arts degree in music theory from Kent State University, where he served as a doctoral assistant. He has taught music theory and designed training materials for the Armed Forces School of Music. He has also taught clarinet, music theory, and composition at the Virginia Governor's School for the Arts and at Tidewater Community College. He has served as an adjudicator for VMTA student and professional composition contests. He is also a senior computer programmer for Unisys Corporation.

John is clarinetist and composer-in-residence for the Hardwick Chamber Ensemble, membership coordinator for the National Association of Composers, USA (NACUSA) and webmaster for the Virginia Music Teachers Association, NACUSA, NACUSA/Virginia, NACUSA/Los Angeles, and the Composer-Conductor Bridge.

John's composition prizes include the 1992 Delius vocal award for *Four Songs*, the 1995 Delius keyboard award for *Three Preludes,* the 1992 VMTA Commissioned Composer Competition prize for *Hardwick*

Quartet, the 1994 VMTA Commissioned Composer Competition prize for *Midas Retold*, and the Modern Music Festival 2000 prize for *Totem*. John has received grants from the American Music Center and *Meet the Composer* and standard awards from ASCAP. His works are frequently performed at new music festivals and conferences throughout the United States. Since 1992, he has received seven commissions from various arts organizations. Recent premieres of his works include the Virginia Beach Chorale's performance of *Jabberwocky* and performances of *Chamber Symphony* and *Decade Divertimento* on the WDR (Cologne) Symphony's chamber music series. The Cologne concert was broadcast on the WDR (West German Radio). Articles by and about John have been published in *ComposerUSA*.

ENDNOTES

1. Carl Sagan, *The Dragons of Eden*, Ballantine Books, New York, 1977, pp. 165–166.

2. Jay Dowling, "Melodic Contour in Hearing and Remembering Melodies," *Musical Perceptions*, Rita Aiello and John A. Sloboda, Eds., Oxford University Press, New York, 1994, pp. 180–184.

3. Diana Deutsch, "Grouping Mechanisms in Music," *The Psychology of Music*, second edition, Diana Deutsch, Ed., Academic Press, San Diego, 1999, p. 301.

4. Diana Deutsch, "Grouping Mechanisms in Music," *The Psychology of Music*, second edition, Diana Deutsch, Ed., Academic Press, San Diego, 1999, pp. 322–323.

5. Diana Deutsch, "The Processing of Pitch Combinations," *The Psychology of Music*, second edition, Diana Deutsch, Ed., Academic Press, San Diego, 1999, p. 357.

6. Diana Deutsch, "The Processing of Pitch Combinations," *The Psychology of Music*, second edition, Diana Deutsch, Ed., Academic Press, San Diego, 1999, p. 399.

7. Diana Deutsch, "Grouping Mechanisms in Music," *The Psychology of Music*, second edition, Diana Deutsch, Ed., Academic Press, San Diego, 1999, p. 314.

8. Leonard Meyer, *Emotion and Meaning in Music*, University of Chicago Press, Chicago, 1956, pp. 157–159.

9. Eric F. Clarke, "Rhythm and Timing in Music," *The Psychology of Music*, second edition, Diana Deutsch, Ed., Academic Press, San Diego, 1999, p. 399.

10. Edward M. Burns, "Intervals, Scales, and Tuning," *The Psychology of Music*, second edition, Diana Deutsch, Ed., Academic Press, San Diego, 1999, p. 257.

11. Leonard Meyer, *Emotion and Meaning in Music*, University of Chicago Press, Chicago, 1956, pp. 22–28.

12. Diana Deutsch, "Grouping Mechanisms in Music," *The Psychology of Music*, second edition, Diana Deutsch, Ed., Academic Press, San Diego, 1999, p. 342.

13. Ian Crofton and Donald Fraser, *A Dictionary of Musical Quotations*, Schirmer Books, New York, 1985, pp. 48–50.

14. Aaron Copland, *What to Listen for in Music*, Penguin books, New York, 1985, p. 34.

15. Leonard Meyer, *Emotion and Meaning in Music*, University of Chicago Press, Chicago, 1956, pp. 1–3.

16. Ian Crofton and Donald Fraser, *A Dictionary of Musical Quotations*, Schirmer Books, New York, 1985, p. 54.

17. Aaron Copland, *Music and Imagination: The Charles Eliot Norton Lectures 1951-1952*, Harvard University Press, Cambridge, 1980, p. 47.

18. Aaron Copland, *Music and Imagination: The Charles Eliot Norton Lectures 1951-1952*, Harvard University Press, Cambridge, 1980: pp. 43–45.

19. Aaron Copland, *What to Listen for in Music*, Penguin books, Inc., New York, 1985, p. 10.

20. Donald J. Grout, *A History of Western Music*, W.W. Norton & Company, 1973, p. 62.

21. Curt Sachs, *The History of Musical Instruments*, W.W. Norton & Company, New York,1940, p. 298.

22. Adam Carse, *The History of Orchestration*, Dover Publications, New York, 1964, pp. 119–126.

23. Charles Wuorinen, "Notes on Performance of Contemporary Music," *Perspectives on Notation and Performance*, Benjamin Boretz and Edward T. Cone, Eds., W.W. Norton & Company, New York, 1976, pp.52–53.

24. Milton Babbitt, "Set Structure as a Compositional Determinant," *Perspectives on Contemporary Music Theory*, Benjamin Boretz and Edward T. Cone, Eds., W.W. Norton & Company, New York, 1972, p. 131.

25. Gardner Read, *Style and Orchestration* (quoting from Berlioz's *Treatise on Instrumentation)*, Schirmer Books, New York, 1979, p. 282.

26. Gardner Read, *Style and Orchestration* (quoting from Schoenberg's *Style and Idea)*, Schirmer Books, New York, 1979, p. 245.

27. Thomas Nagel, "The Sleep of Reason" (a review of *Fashionable Nonsense: Postmodern Intellectuals' Abuse of Science* by Alan Sakal and Jean Bricmont), *The New Republic*, October 12, 1998.

28. Allan Bloom, *The Closing of the American Mind*, Simon and Schuster, New York, 1987. pp. 325–329.

29. Mickie Willis, "Why Do So Many Smart People Listen to Such Terrible Music?" *ComposerUSA*, Spring 2001.

30. Donald Erb, *1997 National Conference Keynote Address*, SCI Newsletter, XXVII:4, April, 1997.

31. Mickie Willis, "Why Do So Many Smart People Listen to Such Terrible Music?" *ComposerUSA*, Spring 2001.

32. Bernard Holland, "Coexisting and Colliding the American Way" (a review of *American Music in the Twentieth Century* by Kyle Gann), *The New York Times*, May 31, 1998.

33. Sheldon Atovsky, "Heterogeneous Schizothymia and the Current Musical Melange: The role of tradition in new music in contemporary society from a European-American composer's point of view," *Chinese Music*, vol. 15, no. 4, December, 1992, pp. 69–76.

34. Nicolas Slonimsky, *Lexicon of Musical Invective*, University of Washington Press, Seattle, 1965, p. 19.

35. Mickie Willis, 'Why Do So Many Smart People Listen to Such Terrible Music?" *ComposerUSA*, Spring 2001.

36. Mark Ryan, "Don't Crossover Beethoven," LM Archives (www.informinc.co.uk/LM/LM112/).

37. Clinton Nieweg, "Composition Competition," (E-Mail entry on Orchestralist listserv), October 27,2000. Refers to Matthew Gurewitsch, "Composers Get a Taste of Direct Democracy," The Wall Street Journal, Tuesday, October 10, 2000, p. A24.

38. Donald Erb, *1997 National Conference Keynote Address*, SCI Newsletter, XXVII:4, April, 1997.

39. Associated Press, "Celebrities should pay for arts, Gingrich says," *The Virginian-Pilot*, Friday, April 1,1997.

40. William F. Buckley, Jr. "The Monuments of Our Society Include Music, Drama and Art," *People for the American Way News*, Winter 1995.

41. Sheldon Atovsky, "Heterogeneous Schizothymia and the Current Musical Melange: The role of tradition in new music in contemporary society from a European-American composer's point of view," *Chinese Music*, vol. 15, no. 4, December, 1992, pp. 69–76.

INDEX

Adams, John, 115-116
Alberti, Domenico, 70
aleatory music, 172
American Composers' Forum, 173
American Symphony Orchestra League, 115
Ars Nova, 59, 101-103, 112
articulations, 28, 36-37, 83
arts funding, 147, 179, 192, 194
Atovsky, Sheldon, v, 153, 202, 216-217
avant-garde, 109, 171-173, 189
Babbitt, Milton, 105, 107, 215
Baby Boomers, 127
Bach, Johann Sebastian1, 53
Barber, Samuel, 116
Baroque Era, 52, 65-67, 72, 82, 94, 168
Bartók, Bela, 99, 176, 204, 210
Beecham, Sir Thomas, 28
Beethoven, Ludwig van, 20-21, 51, 53, 85, 96, 99-100, 115, 118, 164, 217
Berlioz, Hector88, 114
Bernstein, Leonard, 115-116, 152, 204
biological rhythm, 3-5, 31-33, 37, 48, 55, 67, 72, 91, 95-96, 104, 113-114, 147, 179, 208
Bloom, Allan, 128, 216
Boulanger, Nadia, 161
Brahms, Johannes, 85

Printed in the United States
24803LVS00004B/160

9 780595 249985